Thyme-Scented Tenderloin Steaks | page 160

Chipotle Chile Corn Bread | page 64

3

Salad Niçoise | page 208

Mediterranean Beef Stew | page 248

Chicken Gumbo | page 271

Catfish Nuggets with
Tartar Sauce | page 96

6

Grouper with Honey-Citrus Glaze | page 102

Spicy Peanut Pasta | page 239

Slim Sloppy Joes | page 276

Mushroom Barley | page 242

Mexican Black Beans | page 227

10

Linguine with Vegetables and
Asiago Cheese | page 134

Lemon-Raspberry Tarts | page 80

Peach Melba Brûlée | page 83

Chocolate-Banana Smoothie | page 43

Fresh Strawberries with Lime Custard | page 89

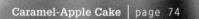

Caramel-Apple Cake | page 74

Peppered Pork with Corn Relish | page 167

Cooking Light.
15-Minute
cookbook

Oxmoor
House.

ISBN: 0-8487-2768-1
Printed in the United States of America
First Printing 2003

Be sure to check with your health-care provider before making any changes in your diet.

Oxmoor House, Inc.

Editor-in-Chief: Nancy Fitzpatrick Wyatt
Executive Editor: Katherine M. Eakin
Art Director: Cynthia R. Cooper
Copy Chief: Allison Long Lowery

Cooking Light® 15-Minute Cookbook

Editor: Heather Averett
Foods Editors: Anne C. Cain, M.P.H., M.S., R.D.; Holley Johnson, M.S., R.D., L.D.
Copy Editors: Jacqueline B. Giovanelli, Diane Rose
Director, Test Kitchens: Elizabeth Tyler Luckett
Assistant Director, Test Kitchens: Julie Christopher
Recipe Editor: Gayle Hays Sadler
Test Kitchens Staff: Kristi Carter, Nicole Faber, Jan A. Smith, Elise Weis, Kelly Wilton
Senior Photographer: Jim Bathie
Photographer: Brit Huckabay
Senior Photo Stylist: Kay E. Clarke
Photo Stylists: Virginia R. Cravens, Ashley J. Wyatt
Publishing Systems Administrator: Rick Tucker
Director, Production and Distribution: Phillip Lee
Production Coordinator: Leslie Johnson
Production Assistant: Faye Porter Bonner

Contributors:
Designer: Carol O. Loria
Indexer: Mary Ann Laurens
Editorial Intern: Terri Laschober
Cover Photographer: Becky Luigart-Stayner
Cover Photo Stylist: Jan Gautro
Cover Recipe Developer: Karen Levin

Cover: Soft Chicken Tacos (recipe on page 181)

To order additional publications, call 1-800-765-6400 or visit oxmoorhouse.com

contents

introduction

Getting dinner on the table quickly just
got easier! The *Cooking Light® 15-Minute Cookbook*
offers you 11 chapters of quick and easy recipes along
with helpful hints for getting dinner on the table in
a snap. Each of the more than 250 kitchen-tested recipes can be
completed from start to finish in approximately 15 minutes (with a
few exceptions for hands-off baking and/or cooking times). We've
included prep and cook times, complete nutrient value information,
and diabetic exchanges for every recipe—for those of you who might
be counting carbohydrates or using exchange lists.

Plus, you'll learn the tricks of the trade from our test kitchens
professionals with "Top 10 Secrets of Fast Food Pros," (page 20) and
the "Stocking Up for Speed," chart (page 22).

Spend less time in the kitchen today...and more time around the table
with friends and family...and good food, too! What are you waiting for?

....

top 10 SECRETS of fast food pros

**If your lifestyle dictates quick, get-it-on-the-table meals,
these 10 tips will make you an expert in superfast cooking.**

1 | Go Ahead and Ask
Quiz family members about their
favorite recipes, even if you already
know what they like. They'll love
having input and smile when their
recipes show up on the plate!

2 | Stock Up on Staples
List the foods and seasonings your family
loves, and have them on hand. Keep a
copy of the list for restocking.

3 | Organize for Speed

You'll be a speed demon in the kitchen if you store things such as mixing bowls, pot holders, spices, and knives in the areas where you use them.

4 | Shop for Tools

Tools for speed cooking low-fat recipes include a nonstick skillet, two or three saucepans, a vegetable steamer, a broiling pan with a rack, good sharp knives, and kitchen scissors.

Kitchen scissors are probably the most helpful for reducing preparation time. Use them for chopping cooked chicken, trimming the fat from meat, chopping fresh herbs over a measuring cup, and cutting dried fruit. Plus, if you use scissors, you won't have to wash a cutting board!

5 | Try Just One

Pick just one new recipe to try instead of several for a single meal. Try an entrée; then serve easy standby recipes for side dishes, or pick up the side dishes and bread at the grocery deli.

6 | Think Ahead

Planning will save you time. No more worrying about the menu as you fight 5 o'clock traffic, or scrounging in the fridge to see what you can cook. In the morning put dinner on in the slow cooker. Or let each family member plan one meal a week.

7 | Do Double Duty

Cook something that requires attention while another recipe simmers or bakes. For example, put on rice to cook before you start cooking the entrée, or chop vegetables while something else simmers.

8 | Make It Easy

Convenience products such as frozen chopped meats and vegetables and canned seasoned vegetable blends save cooking and cleanup time. Look for produce sliced or chopped the way you plan to use it; you'll find the packages in the produce section or precut vegetables in the grocery deli or on the salad bar.

One of the handiest frozen products on the market is seasoning blend. This package of chopped peppers, onions, celery, and parsley can be found in the frozen food section of the supermarket.

Don't forget ready-to-serve pizza crusts; deli-roasted chicken; peeled, cooked shrimp; and spice blends.

9 | Beg, Plead, or Delegate

Or do whatever it takes to get help in the kitchen before and after mealtime. Even 3-year-olds can set out the napkins, and older kids can pour the beverages, set the table, or stir a sauce. Don't forget to encourage help with cleanup, too.

10 | Wipe Out Cleanup

• **Use vegetable cooking spray.** Baked food won't be as hard to clean off casserole dishes and pans if you coat them first.

• **Measure and mix ingredients with cleanup in mind.** For example, measure dry ingredients before wet ones, and you won't have to wash measuring utensils in between measurings.

• **Use disposable products when possible.** Lining baking pans with aluminum foil, and using zip-top plastic bags make cleanup a snap.

stocking up for speed

Here's a list of basic ingredients to keep on hand for cooking healthy, low-fat recipes.

● ●

In the Pantry

CONDIMENTS
Chutney, fruit
Honey
Hot sauce
Jellies, apple, hot pepper
Marmalade, low-sugar orange, low-sugar apricot
Mustard, Dijon
Salsa, tomato
Soy sauce, low-sodium
Syrup, maple
Vinegars, cider, balsamic, red wine
Worcestershire sauce, low-sodium

PASTA AND RICE
Boil-in-bag rice
Brown rice, instant
Couscous, macaroni, spaghetti

CANNED/JARRED PRODUCTS
Beans, black no-salt-added, kidney no-salt-added
Broth, beef no-salt-added, chicken no-salt-added
Corn, whole-kernel no-salt-added
Pasta sauce, low-fat or no-salt-added
Pineapple, slices or tidbits canned in juice
Tomatoes, Cajun-style, Italian-style, Mexican-style, stewed
Tomato sauce, no-salt-added
Tuna, canned in water

MISCELLANEOUS
Cooking spray
Dressing, Italian fat-free
Oils, vegetable and olive
Potatoes, baking and round red
Pound cake, fat-free loaf
Tortilla chips, no-oil, baked

In the Refrigerator

DAIRY
Buttermilk, nonfat
Cream cheese, light or fat-free
Margarine, reduced-calorie
Mayonnaise, reduced-fat or fat-free
Milk, low-fat or fat-free
Sour cream, low-fat or fat-free
Yogurt, plain, fat-free

FRUIT
Apples
Bananas
Grapes
Lemons
Limes
Oranges
Pears
Strawberries

VEGETABLES
Broccoli florets
Cabbage, shredded
Cauliflower florets
Celery
Cucumbers
Green onions
Mushrooms, fresh, sliced
Peppers, green, red, or yellow
Salad greens, package of premixed washed
Spinach, package of washed leaves
Squash, yellow
Tomatoes, regular or plum
Vegetables, package of mixed, cut for stir-fry

MISCELLANEOUS
Garlic, minced, in a jar
Juices, apple, lemon, and orange
Tortillas, fat-free flour
Turkey bacon

In the Freezer

MEAT/POULTRY
Beef, ground round
Chicken, package of frozen chopped, cooked; boneless, skinless chicken breast halves

FRUIT/VEGETABLES
Onions, frozen, chopped
Peaches, frozen, sliced
Peppers, frozen, chopped
Seasoning blend (package of frozen chopped onion, peppers, celery, and parsley)
Strawberries, frozen, sliced or whole

DAIRY
Ice cream, fat-free vanilla
Whipped topping, frozen fat-free
Yogurt, frozen, reduced-fat or fat-free

In the Spice Cabinet
Basil, dried
Chili powder
Cinnamon, ground
Creole seasoning, salt-free
Curry powder
Dill, dried
Garlic powder
Lemon pepper seasoning
Mexican seasoning, salt-free
Mrs. Dash salt-free seasoning blends
Oregano, dried
Pepper, dried crushed red
Pepper, ground, black and red
Rosemary, dried
Thyme, dried
Vanilla extract

healthy substitutions

Use these substitutions to "lighten up" any of your own favorite recipes.

....

Ingredient Needed	Substitution
FATS AND OILS	
Butter or margarine	Reduced-calorie stick margarine or light stick butter in baked products; reduced-calorie margarine, light butter, or yogurt-based spread
Mayonnaise	Fat-free, reduced-fat, or low-fat mayonnaise
Oil	Safflower, soybean, corn, canola, or peanut oil in reduced amount
Salad dressing	Fat-free or oil-free dressing
Shortening	Soybean, corn, canola, or peanut oil in amount reduced by one-third
DAIRY PRODUCTS	
Cheeses: American, Cheddar, colby, Edam or Swiss	Reduced-fat and part-skim cheeses with 5 grams of fat or less per ounce
Cheese, cottage	Fat-free or 1% low-fat cottage cheese
Cheese, cream	Fat-free, ⅓-less-fat, or tub-style light cream cheese
Cheese, ricotta	Fat-free, light, or part-skim ricotta cheese
Cream, sour	Low-fat or fat-free sour cream; low-fat or fat-free yogurt
Cream, whipping	Chilled fat-free evaporated milk or fat-free half-and-half
Ice cream	Fat-free or low-fat frozen yogurt; fat-free or low-fat ice cream; sherbet; sorbet
Milk, whole	Fat-free, low-fat, or reduced-fat milk
MEATS, FISH, POULTRY, AND EGGS	
Bacon	Canadian bacon; turkey bacon; lean ham
Beef, ground	Extralean or ultralean ground beef; freshly ground raw turkey
Beef, lamb, pork, or veal	Chicken, turkey, or lean cuts of meat trimmed of all visible fat
Luncheon meat	Skinned, sliced turkey or chicken breast; lean ham; lean roast beef
Poultry	Skinned poultry
Tuna packed in oil	Tuna packed in water
Turkey, self-basting	Turkey basted with fat-free broth
Egg, whole	2 egg whites or ¼ cup egg substitute
MISCELLANEOUS	
Fudge sauce	Fat-free fudge sauce or chocolate syrup
Nuts	Reduce amount one-third to one-half, and toast
Soups, canned	98%-fat-free or reduced-fat, reduced-sodium condensed cream soups

about these recipes

Cooking Light® *15-Minute Cookbook* gives you the recipe facts you want to know. To make your life easier, we've provided the following useful information with every recipe:

- Prep and cook times
- A complete nutrient analysis per serving
- Diabetic exchange values for those who use them as a guide for planning meals

· ·

Diabetic Exchanges

Exchange values are provided for people who use them for calorie-controlled diets and for people with diabetes. All foods within a certain group contain approximately the same amount of nutrients and calories, so one serving of a food from a food group can be substituted or exchanged for one serving of any other item on the list.

The food groups are starch, fruit, vegetable, milk, meat, and fat. The exchange values are based on the Exchange Lists for Meal Planning developed by the American Diabetes Association and The American Dietetic Association.

Nutritional Analyses

Each recipe offers a complete listing of nutrients; the numbers in the list are based on the following assumptions:

- Unless otherwise indicated, meat, poultry, and fish refer to skinned, boned, and cooked servings.
- When we give a range for an ingredient (3 to 3½ cups flour, for instance), we calculate using the lesser amount.
- Some alcohol calories evaporate during heating; the analysis reflects that.
- Only the amount of marinade absorbed by the food is used in calculation.
- Garnishes and optional ingredients are not included in analysis.

The nutritional values used in our calculations come from computer programs by Computrition, Inc., and The Food Processor, Version 7.5 (ESHA Research), or are provided by food manufacturers.

appetizers & beverages

• make ahead • vegetarian •

Baked Pita Chips

prep: 5 minutes   cook: 12 minutes

Experiment with your favorite seasonings for these easy homemade chips. Serve them with Garlic-Herb Cheese Spread (recipe on page 32).

4   (6-inch) pitas
Garlic- or olive oil-flavored cooking spray

Preheat oven to 350°.
Cut each pita round into 8 wedges; separate each wedge into 2 wedges. Place wedges in a single layer on 2 baking sheets; coat wedges with cooking spray. Bake at 350° for 12 to 13 minutes or until lightly browned. Let cool. Store in an airtight container.
Yield: 8 servings (serving size: 8 chips).

Per Serving: Calories **88** Fat **0.8g** (sat **0.0g**) Protein **1.6g** Carbohydrate **16.0g** Fiber **3.2g**
Cholesterol **0mg** Iron **0.8mg** Sodium **184mg** Calcium **24mg**
Exchange: 1 Starch

Italian-Flavored Pita Chips

Coat pita wedges with cooking spray, and sprinkle with ⅛ teaspoon garlic powder and ¼ teaspoon dried Italian seasoning. Bake at 350° for 12 to 13 minutes or until lightly browned. Let cool. Store in an airtight container.

Fresh Tomato Salsa

prep: 15 minutes

Seeding the tomatoes prevents the salsa from being watery. To seed a tomato, cut it in half horizontally, and scoop out the seeds with a spoon.

3   cups chopped seeded tomato (about 3 large)
½   cup chopped red onion (about 1 small)
3   tablespoons minced fresh cilantro
3   tablespoons fresh lime juice (about 2 limes)
½   teaspoon salt
2   garlic cloves, minced
1   jalapeño pepper, seeded and chopped

Combine all ingredients in a medium bowl.
Yield: 2 cups (serving size: 1 tablespoon).

Per Serving: Calories **4** Fat **0.0g** (sat **0.0g**) Protein **0.2g** Carbohydrate **0.9g** Fiber **0.2g**
Cholesterol **0mg** Iron **0.1mg** Sodium **38mg** Calcium **2mg**
Exchange: Free (up to ⅓ cup)

Classic Onion Dip

prep: 5 minutes   chill: 1 hour

Serve this dip with raw vegetables, Melba toast rounds, or crackers.

1   (8-ounce) carton fat-free sour cream
½   cup finely chopped onion (about 1 small)
2   teaspoons low-sodium soy sauce
¼   teaspoon garlic pepper (such as Lawry's)

Combine all ingredients in a medium bowl; stir well. Cover and chill 1 hour.
Yield: 1 cup (serving size: 1 tablespoon).

Per Serving: Calories **12** Fat **0.0g** (sat **0.0g**) Protein **1.1g** Carbohydrate **1.4g** Fiber **0.1g**
Cholesterol **0mg** Iron **0.0mg** Sodium **40mg** Calcium **21mg**
Exchange: Free (up to 3 tablespoons)

• make ahead • vegetarian •

Guacamole

prep: 15 minutes

Fresh lime juice gives this guacamole a tart flavor. For added pizzazz, decrease the lime juice to 1 to 2 tablespoons, and add a few drops of hot sauce. Serve this classic dip with baked tortilla chips.

1   cup diced peeled avocado (about 1 medium)
6   ounces firm, silken-style tofu, drained and cubed
1   (4.5-ounce) can chopped green chiles, drained
½   cup chopped green onions (about 4)
¼   cup fat-free mayonnaise
2   tablespoons chopped fresh parsley
2   tablespoons minced fresh cilantro
3   to 4 tablespoons fresh lime juice (about 2 limes)
¾   teaspoon salt
2   garlic cloves, halved
1   jalapeño pepper, seeded

Place all ingredients in a food processor; process until smooth, scraping down sides if necessary. Spoon mixture into a bowl; cover and chill.

Yield: 2 cups (serving size: 1 tablespoon).

Per Serving: Calories **17**   Fat **1.2g** (sat **0.2g**)   Protein **0.6g**   Carbohydrate **1.4g**   Fiber **0.5g**
Cholesterol **0mg**   Iron **0.4mg**   Sodium **120mg**   Calcium **8mg**
Exchange: Free (up to 2 tablespoons)

• make ahead • vegetarian •

Hummus

prep: 12 minutes

*This traditional Middle Eastern purée of garbanzo beans and garlic is
delicious as a dip with pita wedges or baked tortilla chips. Try a flavor
variation of this tasty spread by adding ½ cup bottled roasted red bell
peppers, drained and chopped, to the bean mixture before processing.*

1	(15½-ounce) can chickpeas (garbanzo beans)
3	tablespoons lemon juice
2	tablespoons chopped green onions (about 1 small)
1	tablespoon tahini (sesame-seed paste)
½	teaspoon salt
¼	teaspoon hot sauce
1	to 2 garlic cloves, minced

Drain beans, reserving ¼ cup liquid.
Combine beans, reserved liquid, and remaining ingredients in a
blender; process until smooth. Cover and chill.
Yield: 1 cup (serving size: 1 tablespoon).

Per Serving: Calories **32**   Fat **0.7g** (sat **0.1g**)   Protein **1.2g**   Carbohydrate **5.4g**   Fiber **1.5g**
Cholesterol **0mg**   Iron **0.4mg**   Sodium **138mg**   Calcium **12mg**
Exchange: ½ Starch

Blue Cheese-Bean Dip

prep: 5 minutes   cook: 6 minutes

Featuring a dusting of breadcrumbs and parsley, this dip is best served with Melba toast rounds, pita wedges, or no-oil-baked tortilla chips.

⅓   cup evaporated fat-free milk
½   teaspoon dried thyme
½   teaspoon freshly ground black pepper
¼   teaspoon ground sage
¼   teaspoon salt
2   (16-ounce) cans cannellini beans, rinsed and drained
2   garlic cloves, sliced
½   cup (2 ounces) crumbled blue cheese
1   tablespoon grated Parmesan cheese
Cooking spray
½   cup dry breadcrumbs
2   tablespoons chopped fresh parsley

Place first 7 ingredients in a food processor; process until smooth. Stir in cheeses.
Spoon bean mixture into a shallow 1-quart baking dish coated with cooking spray. Cover with heavy-duty plastic wrap, and vent; microwave at HIGH 6 minutes, stirring every 2 minutes.
Combine breadcrumbs and parsley; sprinkle over bean mixture.
Yield: 3 cups (serving size: 1 tablespoon).

Per Serving: Calories **17**   Fat **0.4g** (sat **0.3g**)   Protein **1.0g**   Carbohydrate **2.1g**   Fiber **0.3g**
Cholesterol **1mg**   Iron **0.2mg**   Sodium **52mg**   Calcium **16mg**
Exchange: Free (up to ¼ cup)

Mexican Sour Cream Dip with Mixed Vegetables

prep: 12 minutes

We suggest serving this spicy dip with cucumber, red bell pepper, and squash. But for a variation, serve over a baked potato stuffed with plenty of steamed vegetables.

1   cup reduced-fat sour cream
1½ tablespoons lime juice
1   tablespoon extravirgin olive oil
2   tablespoons chopped fresh cilantro
½   teaspoon ground cumin
¼   teaspoon ground red pepper
¼   teaspoon salt
1   (8-ounce) cucumber, cut into 16 slices
1   (6-ounce) red bell pepper, cut into 16 strips
1   (8-ounce) squash, cut into 16 slices

Combine first 7 ingredients in a small bowl; stir until well blended. Serve with vegetables.

Yield: 6 servings (serving size: about 3½ tablespoons dip and 8 vegetable pieces).

Per Serving: Calories **88**   Fat **4.4g** (sat **1.7g**)   Protein **3.1g**   Carbohydrate **9.1g**   Fiber **1.4g**
Cholesterol **8mg**   Iron **0.8mg**   Sodium **146mg**   Calcium **63mg**
Exchanges: ½ Starch, ½ Vegetable, 1 Fat

• make ahead • vegetarian •

Garlic-Herb Cheese Spread

prep: 12 minutes   chill: 1 hour

Garlic and fresh herbs make this stir-and-chill dip taste garden fresh. The chilling time is important because it gives the flavors a chance to blend. Serve with Baked Pita Chips (recipe on page 26).

1½ cups fat-free sour cream
½   cup (4 ounces) block-style light cream cheese
1   tablespoon minced fresh chives
2   teaspoons minced fresh parsley
½   teaspoon salt
½   teaspoon freshly ground black pepper
1   small garlic clove, minced, or ½ teaspoon bottled minced garlic

Combine sour cream and cream cheese in a bowl; stir well. Stir in chives and remaining ingredients; cover and chill at least 1 hour.

Yield: 2 cups (serving size: 1 tablespoon).

Per Serving: Calories **16**   Fat **0.6g** (sat **0.4g**)   Protein **1.2g**   Carbohydrate **1.1g**   Fiber **0.0g**
Cholesterol **2mg**   Iron **0.0mg**   Sodium **65mg**   Calcium **18mg**
Exchange: Free (up to ⅓ cup)

Asian Lettuce Wraps

prep: 15 minutes

Packaged coleslaw mix keeps prep time to a minimum; look for it in your grocer's produce department.

1   tablespoon plus 1 teaspoon reduced-fat crunchy peanut butter
1½   teaspoons honey
1½   teaspoons cider vinegar
1½   teaspoons low-sodium soy sauce
¼   teaspoon curry powder
⅛   teaspoon ground red pepper
1   (16-ounce) package coleslaw mix
4   leaves iceberg lettuce or napa (Chinese) cabbage
4   thin slices deli-style turkey breast

Combine first 6 ingredients in a medium bowl; stir well. Add coleslaw; toss to coat.

Place one slice of turkey on each lettuce leaf; top with ½ cup coleslaw mixture. Roll up; secure each end with a wooden pick. Cut each wrap in half diagonally.

Yield: 4 servings (serving size: 2 halves).

Per Serving: Calories **85** Fat **2.5g** (sat **0.6g**) Protein **9.2g** Carbohydrate **7.5g** Fiber **1.5g**
Cholesterol **16mg** Iron **0.8mg** Sodium **380mg** Calcium **25mg**
Exchanges: ½ Starch, ½ Vegetable, 1 Very Lean Meat

Mediterranean Nachos

prep: 15 minutes   cook: 5 minutes

The easiest way to cut pita bread into wedges is with a pizza cutter or kitchen shears.

2   (6-inch) pitas
Cooking spray
¼   teaspoon salt
1   (15½-ounce) can chickpeas (garbanzo beans), drained
¼   cup sliced green onions (about 2)
2   tablespoons lemon juice
1   tablespoon fat-free milk
1   teaspoon olive oil
2   garlic cloves
1   cup chopped tomato (about 1 medium)
3   tablespoons chopped ripe olives

Preheat oven to 450°.
Separate each pita bread round into 2 rounds; cut each round into 6 wedges. Place wedges on a large baking sheet; coat wedges with cooking spray, and sprinkle evenly with salt. Bake at 450° for 5 minutes or until lightly browned.
While pita wedges bake, place beans and next 5 ingredients in a food processor; process until smooth, scraping sides of bowl once.
Spread 2 teaspoons bean mixture over each pita wedge; sprinkle wedges evenly with chopped tomato and olives. Serve nachos immediately.
Yield: 24 appetizers (serving size: 1 appetizer).

Per Serving: Calories **32**   Fat **0.6g** (sat **0.1g**)   Protein **1.0g**   Carbohydrate **5.7g**   Fiber **1.4g**
Cholesterol **0mg**   Iron **0.4mg**   Sodium **76mg**   Calcium **11mg**
Exchange: ½ Starch

• make ahead • vegetarian •

Roasted Red Pepper and Ripe Olive Crostini

prep: 15 minutes   cook: 15 minutes   stand: 15 minutes

This easy appetizer can be prepared ahead. Assemble the red pepper-olive mixture, cover it with plastic wrap, and store it in the refrigerator for up to 8 hours. Then, spoon the mixture on the baguette slices before serving.

16 (¼-inch-thick) slices diagonally cut French bread baguette
Cooking spray
1   tablespoon dried basil, divided
1   (4¼-ounce) can chopped ripe olives, drained
1½ tablespoons red wine vinegar
½   teaspoon minced garlic (about ½ clove)
¼   cup (1 ounce) crumbled feta cheese with basil and sun-dried
        tomatoes
1   (15½-ounce) bottle roasted red bell peppers, drained and finely
        chopped

Preheat oven to 350°.
Place bread slices on a baking sheet; coat with cooking spray, and sprinkle evenly with 1½ teaspoons basil. Bake at 350° for 15 minutes or until golden and crispy. Remove bread slices from baking sheet to a wire rack; let cool completely.
Combine olives, remaining basil, vinegar, and garlic in a small bowl; gently stir in cheese and peppers. Let stand 15 minutes.
Spoon 2 tablespoons olive mixture onto each bread slice.
Yield: 16 servings (serving size: 1 crostino).

Per Serving: Calories **45**   Fat **1.5g** (sat **0.5g**)   Protein **1.1g**   Carbohydrate **5.6g**   Fiber **0.5g**
Cholesterol **1mg**   Iron **0.5mg**   Sodium **223mg**   Calcium **23mg**
Exchange: ½ Starch

Chicken and Green Chile Quesadillas

prep: 15 minutes   cook: 12 minutes

Serve these creamy quesadillas with Guacamole (recipe on page 28)
and Fresh Tomato Salsa (recipe on page 27).

6   (8-inch) flour tortillas
¾   cup light cream cheese with garlic and spices or light cream
        cheese
2   roasted skinless, boneless chicken breast halves (such as Tyson),
        thinly sliced
2   (4.5-ounce) cans chopped green chiles, drained
⅓   cup finely chopped red onion (about ½ small)
Cooking spray

Spread each tortilla with 2 tablespoons cream cheese. Top evenly with
chicken, chiles, and onion. Fold tortillas in half.
Coat a large nonstick skillet with cooking spray; place over medium
heat until hot. Add tortillas, two at a time, and cook 1 minute on each
side or until golden. Cut each quesadilla in half. Serve warm.
Yield: 12 servings (serving size: ½ quesadilla).

Per Serving: Calories **134** Fat **4.5g** (sat **2.2g**) Protein **9.2g** Carbohydrate **14.0g** Fiber **0.9g**
Cholesterol **21mg** Iron **0.8mg** Sodium **514mg** Calcium **44mg**
Exchanges: 1 Starch, 1 Medium-Fat Meat

Black Bean Cakes

prep: 12 minutes   cook: 4 minutes

Garlic and cumin give these bean cakes a bold, earthy flavor.

1	(15-ounce) can black beans, rinsed and drained
2	tablespoons no-salt-added tomato paste
2	garlic cloves, minced
1½	teaspoons ground cumin, divided
¼	teaspoon salt
2	tablespoons dry breadcrumbs
½	teaspoon freshly ground black pepper
	Olive oil-flavored cooking spray
2	teaspoons olive oil
¼	cup salsa
¼	cup fat-free sour cream
	Chopped fresh cilantro (optional)

Combine first 3 ingredients, ½ teaspoon cumin, and salt in a large bowl; mash with a fork. Divide mixture evenly into 8 portions. Shape into 8 balls; set aside.

Combine breadcrumbs, pepper, and remaining 1 teaspoon cumin in a shallow dish. Roll balls in crumb mixture. Shape into ½-inch-thick patties.

Coat a large nonstick skillet with cooking spray; add oil. Place over medium-high heat until hot. Add patties; cook 2 minutes on each side or until lightly browned.

To serve, place 1 bean cake on each of 8 serving plates. Top each with 1½ teaspoons salsa and 1½ teaspoons sour cream. Garnish with cilantro, if desired. Serve immediately.

Yield: 8 servings.

Per Serving: Calories **79**   Fat **1.6g** (sat **0.2g**)   Protein **4.4g**   Carbohydrate **12.2g**   Fiber **2.0g**
Cholesterol **0mg**   Iron **1.2mg**   Sodium **194mg**   Calcium **29mg**
Exchange: 1 Starch

Candy Apple Cider

prep: 5 minutes

When buying fresh ginger, look for smooth skin (wrinkled skin indicates that the root is dry and past its prime). Also, the ginger should have a fresh, spicy fragrance.

4   cups apple cider
2   tablespoons red cinnamon candies
1   (1-inch) piece peeled fresh ginger
4   (3-inch) cinnamon sticks (optional)

Combine first 3 ingredients in a medium saucepan. Bring mixture to a boil; reduce heat and simmer, stirring constantly, until candy melts. Remove and discard ginger.

To serve, pour into individual mugs. Garnish with a cinnamon stick, if desired. Serve immediately.

Yield: 4 servings (serving size: 1 cup).

Per Serving: Calories **156**   Fat **0.2g** (sat **0.0g**)   Protein **0.1g**   Carbohydrate **39.4g**   Fiber **0.5g**
Cholesterol **0mg**   Iron **0.9mg**   Sodium **11mg**   Calcium **18mg**
Exchanges: ½ Starch, 2 Fruit

• make ahead •

Tropical Peach Punch

prep: 10 minutes

The juice mixture can easily be made a day in advance. Cover and store it in the refrigerator; add the ginger ale just before serving.

2   cups coarsely chopped peeled peaches (about 4)
1½ cups orange-pineapple juice
½   cup frozen white grape juice concentrate
2   cups sugar-free ginger ale

Combine first 3 ingredients in a blender; process until smooth, stopping once to scrape down sides.
Fill 4 tall glasses with crushed ice; add 1 cup juice mixture and ½ cup ginger ale to each glass. Stir gently; serve immediately.
Yield: 4 servings (serving size: 1½ cups).

Per Serving: Calories 190 Fat **0.1g** (sat **0.0g**) Protein **1.2g** Carbohydrate **47.1g** Fiber **2.4g**
Cholesterol **0mg** Iron **0.1mg** Sodium **41mg** Calcium **6mg**
Exchanges: ½ Starch, 2½ Fruit

Cranberry-Citrus Spritzer

prep: 5 minutes

While fruit juices aren't rich in fiber like whole fruits, they're good sources of other nutrients. This spritzer is a great source of vitamin C.

2¾ cups cranberry juice cocktail, chilled
¾   cup citrus punch, chilled (such as Minute Maid)
2½ cups sugar-free lemon-lime soda, chilled

Combine all ingredients in a large bowl; stir well. Serve immediately.
Yield: 6 servings (serving size: 1 cup).

Per Serving: Calories 79 Fat **0.0g** (sat **0.0g**) Protein **0.0g** Carbohydrate **19.6g** Fiber **0.0g**
Cholesterol **0mg** Iron **0.2mg** Sodium **29mg** Calcium **13mg**
Exchanges: ½ Starch, 1 Fruit

Mint Limeade

prep: 8 minutes   chill: 1 hour

Enhance the flavor of this summertime treat by serving it with citrus-mint ice cubes. Simply place a small mint sprig and a lime slice in each section of ice cube trays; add sugar-free lemon-lime soft drink. Freeze until firm.

2   cups boiling water
2   mint tea bags
2   (6-ounce) cans limeade concentrate, undiluted

Combine water and tea bags in a 2-cup glass measure; cover and steep 7 minutes. Remove and discard tea bags. Cool to room temperature. **Combine** limeade and 2 cans of water in a 2-quart pitcher; add tea, stirring well. Cover and chill. Serve over crushed ice, if desired.

Yield: 7 servings (serving size: 1 cup).

Per Serving: Calories **92**   Fat **0.0g** (sat **0.0g**)   Protein **0.1g**   Carbohydrate **24.3g**   Fiber **0.0g**
Cholesterol **0mg**   Iron **0.3mg**   Sodium **2mg**   Calcium **2mg**
Exchanges: 1½ Starch

Sunrise Slush

prep: 8 minutes

½   (12-ounce) container frozen orange-strawberry-banana juice
        concentrate
1   (6-ounce) can unsweetened pineapple juice
3   cups ice cubes

Combine all ingredients in a blender; process until smooth, stopping once to scrape down sides.
Serve immediately.

Yield: 4 servings (serving size: 1 cup).

Per Serving: Calories **121**   Fat **0.0g** (sat **0.0g**)   Protein **0.9g**   Carbohydrate **28.4g**   Fiber **0.0g**
Cholesterol **0mg**   Iron **0.1mg**   Sodium **23mg**   Calcium **7mg**
Exchanges: 2 Fruit

Strawberry-Cherry Slush

prep: 5 minutes

Don't thaw the strawberries and cherries; processing the frozen berries is what makes the beverage slushy. We used cherry-flavored 7-Up for the soda, but you can substitute any other clear carbonated soda.

1⅓ cups frozen dark pitted sweet cherries
1 cup frozen unsweetened whole strawberries
1 cup cherry-flavored lemon-lime soda, chilled
2 tablespoons sugar
2 tablespoons frozen reduced-calorie whipped topping, thawed
1 tablespoon fresh lemon juice (about 1 lemon)

Combine all ingredients in a blender; process until smooth, stopping twice to scrape down sides. Pour into tall chilled glasses. Serve immediately.

Yield: 2¼ cups (serving size: ¾ cup).

Per Serving: Calories **120** Fat **0.7g** (sat **0.2g**) Protein **0.9g** Carbohydrate **29.7g** Fiber **0.6g** Cholesterol **0mg** Iron **0.7mg** Sodium **12mg** Calcium **18mg**
Exchanges: 2 Fruit

Dreamy Orange Smoothie

prep: 5 minutes

2 cups orange sherbet
2 cups vanilla reduced-fat ice cream
½ cup 1% low-fat milk

Combine all ingredients in a blender; process until thick and smooth. **Pour** into glasses, and serve immediately.

Yield: 4 servings (serving size: 1 cup).

Per Serving: Calories **259** Fat **4.3g** (sat **2.3g**) Protein **5.1g** Carbohydrate **50.1g** Fiber **1.0g** Cholesterol **12mg** Iron **0.2mg** Sodium **106mg** Calcium **191mg**
Exchanges: 3 Starch

Strawberry Smoothie

prep: 5 minutes

If mango isn't available, substitute half of a banana or increase the strawberries to 2 cups.

1½ cups halved strawberries
1   (8-ounce) carton strawberry-banana low-fat yogurt
½   cup cubed peeled ripe mango
⅓   cup pineapple juice
2   tablespoons honey
Ice cubes
4   whole strawberries

Combine first 5 ingredients in a blender; process until smooth.
Add enough ice cubes to bring mixture to 5-cup level; process until smooth.
To serve, pour into glasses. Garnish with whole strawberries. Serve immediately.
Yield: 4 servings (serving size: 1¼ cups).

Per Serving: Calories **140** Fat **1.0g** (sat **0.4g**) Protein **3.0g** Carbohydrate **31.8g** Fiber **2.4g**
Cholesterol **2mg** Iron **0.5mg** Sodium **32mg** Calcium **97mg**
Exchanges: 1 Starch, 1 Fruit

Banana-Berry Smoothie

prep: 5 minutes

This treat is so thick and creamy that you'll need to serve it with a spoon.

1   cup frozen unsweetened whole strawberries
1   small banana (about 5 ounces)
¼   cup fat-free milk
1   cup vanilla fat-free ice cream
Banana slices (optional)

Combine first 3 ingredients in a blender; process until smooth, stopping once to scrape down sides. Add ice cream; blend until smooth. Garnish with banana slices, if desired, and serve immediately.
Yield: 2 servings (serving size: 1 cup).

Per Serving: Calories **202** Fat **0.4g** (sat **0.2g**) Protein **5.1g** Carbohydrate **47.9g** Fiber **2.7g**
Cholesterol **1mg** Iron **0.8mg** Sodium **63mg** Calcium **54mg**
Exchanges: 2 Starch, 1 Fruit

Chocolate-Banana Smoothie *(photo, page 14)*

prep: 5 minutes

1   cup frozen sliced banana (about 1 large)
2   cups 1% chocolate low-fat milk
⅔   cup chocolate fudge fat-free, no-sugar-added ice cream (such as Edy's)
Chocolate shavings (optional)

Combine first 3 ingredients in a blender. Process until smooth, stopping once to scrape down sides. Garnish with chocolate shavings, if desired, and serve immediately.
Yield: 3 servings (serving size: about 1 cup).

Per Serving: Calories **204** Fat **1.9g** (sat **1.1g**) Protein **7.6g** Carbohydrate **40.8g** Fiber **1.6g**
Cholesterol **7mg** Iron **0.7mg** Sodium **147mg** Calcium **205mg**
Exchanges: 1 Starch, 1 Fruit, 1 Skim Milk

Creamy Hot Cocoa Mix

prep: 5 minutes

Savor the intense flavor of chocolate in this creamy, satisfying hot cocoa mix. Scoop only the amount you need, and store the remainder in an airtight container.

1 (15-ounce) can instant chocolate milk mix (such as Nesquick)
1 (11-ounce) jar powdered nondairy coffee creamer
1⅓ cups sifted powdered sugar
1 (9.6-ounce) package instant nonfat dry milk
1 cup unsweetened cocoa

Combine all ingredients in a large bowl; store in an airtight container in a cool place.
Yield: 10⅓ cups (serving size: ⅓ cup).

Per Serving: Calories **168** Fat **3.2g** (sat **3.0g**) Protein **4.6g** Carbohydrate **27.5g** Fiber **0.6g**
Cholesterol **11mg** Iron **3.0mg** Sodium **285mg** Calcium **679mg**
Exchanges: 2 Starch, ½ Fat

Cocoa by the Cup

NUMBER OF 1-CUP SERVINGS	HOT COCOA MIX	BOILING WATER
1	⅓ cup	1 cup
2	⅔ cup	2 cups
4	1⅓ cups	4 cups

breads

Raisin Bread French Toast *(photo, page 3)*

prep: 2 minutes   cook: 8 minutes

Keep cinnamon-raisin bread on hand for this no-fuss French toast. You can have this breakfast treat on the table in about 10 minutes flat.

½   cup egg substitute
¼   cup fat-free milk
½   teaspoon vanilla extract
¼   teaspoon ground cinnamon
Cooking spray
8   slices cinnamon-raisin bread
2   teaspoons sifted powdered sugar
½   cup reduced-calorie maple syrup

Combine first 4 ingredients in a shallow bowl, stirring well.
Coat a large nonstick skillet with cooking spray; place pan over medium heat until hot.
Dip bread slices into egg substitute mixture, coating sides well. Place 4 slices in pan; cook 2 minutes on each side or until lightly browned. Remove from pan; sprinkle with half of powdered sugar.
Repeat with remaining bread slices and sugar. Serve with syrup.
Yield: 4 servings (serving size: 2 slices bread and 2 tablespoons syrup).

Per Serving: Calories **171**   Fat **1.5g** (sat **0.3g**)   Protein **6.8g**   Carbohydrate **33.4g**   Fiber **1.9g**
Cholesterol **2mg**   Iron **1.2mg**   Sodium **243mg**   Calcium **66mg**
Exchanges: 2 Starch

Parmesan Bruschetta

prep: 5 minutes   cook: 1 minute

A sharp knife with a serrated edge or an electric knife will help you cut clean slices from a fresh, soft loaf of bread.

4	tablespoons grated Parmesan cheese
4	tablespoons (2 ounces) light cream cheese
½	teaspoon garlic powder
½	teaspoon dried Italian seasoning
8	(½-inch-thick) diagonally cut slices Italian bread

Preheat broiler.

Combine first 4 ingredients in a small bowl; stir well. Spread cheese mixture evenly over bread slices.

Place bread slices on a baking sheet; broil 1 minute or until toasted.

Yield: 8 servings (serving size: 1 slice).

Per Serving: Calories **92**   Fat **2.5g** (sat **0.4g**)   Protein **4.2g**   Carbohydrate **12.8g**   Fiber **0.6g**
Cholesterol **7mg**   Iron **0.6mg**   Sodium **230mg**   Calcium **63mg**
Exchange: 1 Starch

Peppered Pimiento-Cheese Bread

prep: 11 minutes   cook: 8 minutes

If you love pimiento and cheese sandwiches, you're sure to be a fan of this yummy, cheesy bread.

¾   cup (3 ounces) preshredded fat-free Cheddar and mozzarella
      cheese blend
½   cup fat-free mayonnaise
3   tablespoons chopped green onions (1 large)
2   tablespoons diced pimiento
½   teaspoon seasoned pepper
2   (2½-ounce) submarine rolls, halved lengthwise

Preheat oven to 400°.

Combine first 5 ingredients, stirring well.

Cut each roll in half crosswise. Spread cheese mixture evenly over cut sides of rolls. Place rolls on a baking sheet; bake at 400° for 8 minutes or until cheese melts.

Yield: 8 slices (serving size: 1 slice).

Per Serving: Calories **72**   Fat **0.4g** (sat **0.1g**)   Protein **5.3g**   Carbohydrate **12.9g**   Fiber **0.6g**
Cholesterol **0mg**   Iron **0.5mg**   Sodium **369mg**   Calcium **59mg**
Exchange: 1 Starch

Tomato-Parmesan Flatbread

prep: 7 minutes   cook: 15 minutes

Make your own garlic-herb Parmesan cheese by combining 2 tablespoons regular grated Parmesan cheese, 1/2 teaspoon dried Italian seasoning, and 1/8 teaspoon garlic powder.

2   tablespoons sun-dried tomato sprinkles (packed without oil)
1½ tablespoons fat-free Caesar Italian dressing
1   (11.3-ounce) can refrigerated dinner roll dough
2   tablespoons grated garlic-herb Parmesan cheese blend
Cooking spray

Preheat oven to 375°.
Combine tomato sprinkles and dressing in a small bowl; let mixture stand 5 minutes.
While tomato mixture stands, remove roll dough from package; separate into rolls. Roll each piece into a 4-inch round.
Brush rounds evenly with tomato mixture, and sprinkle evenly with Parmesan cheese blend. Place rounds on a baking sheet coated with cooking spray. Bake at 375° for 15 minutes or until golden.
Yield: 8 servings (serving size: 1 flatbread).

Per Serving: Calories **129**   Fat **2.1g** (sat **0.0g**)   Protein **4.3g**   Carbohydrate **20.8g**   Fiber **0.3g**
Cholesterol **0mg**   Iron **0.1mg**   Sodium **393mg**   Calcium **3mg**
Exchanges: 1½ Starch, ½ Fat

Strawberry-Almond Danish

prep: 13 minutes   cook: 10 minutes

*Parchment paper eliminates the need for greasing the baking sheet, so
cleanup is easy. You can spray the baking sheet with cooking spray if
you prefer.*

1/4   cup (2 ounces) block-style fat-free cream cheese
1   tablespoon sifted powdered sugar
1/8   teaspoon almond extract
1   (8-ounce) can refrigerated reduced-fat crescent dinner roll dough
2   tablespoons strawberry spread (such as Polaner All Fruit)
1/3   cup plus 1 tablespoon sifted powdered sugar
2   teaspoons fat-free milk

Preheat oven to 375°.
Combine first 3 ingredients, stirring until smooth; set aside.
Unroll dough; separate into 8 triangles. Spoon 1 heaping teaspoon
cream cheese mixture onto wide part of each crescent roll. Dollop
strawberry spread evenly over cream cheese mixture. Roll crescents
according to package directions, pinching ends of crescents.
Place rolls, point sides down, on a baking sheet lined with parchment
paper. Bake at 375° for 10 minutes or until golden.
Combine 1/3 cup plus 1 tablespoon powdered sugar and milk; stir well.
Drizzle over crescents.
Yield: 8 servings (serving size: 1 Danish).

Per Serving: Calories **135** Fat **4.5g** (sat **1.0g**) Protein **3.2g** Carbohydrate **19.9g** Fiber **0.0g**
Cholesterol **1mg** Iron **0.1mg** Sodium **279mg** Calcium **24mg**
Exchanges: 1 Starch, 1 Fat

Sticky Buns

prep: 10 minutes   cook: 12 minutes   stand: 1 minute

When you chop pecans for this recipe, chop extra to freeze and have on hand to use in other recipes.

¼   cup packed dark brown sugar
3   tablespoons reduced-calorie stick margarine, divided
¼   cup apple juice
Cooking spray
2   tablespoons finely chopped pecans
2   tablespoons granulated sugar
½   teaspoon ground cinnamon
¼   cup currants
1   (10.8-ounce) can refrigerated reduced-calorie biscuit dough

Combine brown sugar, 2 tablespoons margarine, and apple juice in a small saucepan. Bring to a boil; reduce heat, and simmer, uncovered, 8 minutes or until slightly thickened. Pour syrup evenly into 8 muffin cups coated with cooking spray; sprinkle with pecans, and set pans aside.
Preheat oven to 375°.
Combine sugar, cinnamon, and currants in a small bowl; toss well to coat currants. Set aside.
Roll biscuits onto a lightly floured surface into a 12 x 9-inch rectangle. Spread dough with remaining 1 tablespoon margarine, and sprinkle with currant mixture to within ¼ inch of edge. Roll up dough, starting at short side. Pinch seam to seal (do not seal ends). Cut dough into 8 slices. Place cut sides of slices on top of pecan mixture in muffin cups. Bake at 375° for 12 minutes or until golden. Invert buns onto a serving plate; let buns stand, covered with muffin pans, 1 minute. Remove from pans, scraping any remaining pecan mixture from pans onto buns. Serve buns warm.
Yield: 8 buns (serving size: 1 bun).

Per Serving: Calories **215**   Fat **8.6g** (sat **1.0g**)   Protein **2.9g**   Carbohydrate **32.6g**   Fiber **0.2g**
Cholesterol **0mg**   Iron **0.4mg**   Sodium **435mg**   Calcium **15mg**
Exchanges: 1 Starch, 1 Fat

Light Mayonnaise Rolls

prep: 5 minutes   cook: 12 minutes

Substitute 1 cup all-purpose flour plus 1 teaspoon baking powder and ½ teaspoon salt in place of 1 cup self-rising flour.

1   cup self-rising flour
3   tablespoons light mayonnaise
½   cup fat-free milk
Cooking spray

Preheat oven to 425°.
Combine first 3 ingredients, stirring just until flour is moistened. Spoon batter into muffin cups coated with cooking spray, filling two-thirds full.
Bake at 425° for 12 minutes or until rolls are lightly browned. Remove from pans immediately.
Yield: 6 rolls (serving size: 1 roll).

Per Serving: Calories **103**   Fat **2.5g** (sat **0.1g**)   Protein **2.8g**   Carbohydrate **16.9g**   Fiber **0.0g**
Cholesterol **3mg**   Iron **1.0mg**   Sodium **331mg**   Calcium **96mg**
Exchanges: 1 Starch, ½ Fat

Bacon-Cheese Drop Biscuits *(photo, page 3)*

prep: 10 minutes   cook: 10 minutes

An ounce of turkey bacon has two-thirds less fat than an ounce of regular bacon.

2   turkey-bacon slices
2   cups low-fat baking mix (such as reduced-fat Bisquick)
½   cup (2 ounces) preshredded reduced-fat sharp Cheddar cheese
2   tablespoons chopped green onions (about 1)
⅛   teaspoon ground red pepper
¾   cup fat-free milk
Cooking spray

Preheat oven to 400°.
Place bacon on a microwave-safe plate lined with paper towels. Microwave at HIGH 1½ minutes. Crumble bacon.
Combine bacon, biscuit mix, and next 3 ingredients, stirring mixture well. Add milk, stirring just until dry ingredients are moist. Drop dough by rounded tablespoonfuls, 2 inches apart, onto a large baking sheet coated with cooking spray.
Bake at 400° for 10 to 12 minutes or until golden. Serve immediately.
Yield: 16 biscuits (serving size: 1 biscuit).

Per Serving: Calories **75** Fat **1.9g** (sat **0.7g**) Protein **2.8g** Carbohydrate **11.3g** Fiber **0.0g**
Cholesterol **4mg** Iron **0.1mg** Sodium **229mg** Calcium **49mg**
Exchange: 1 Starch

Cream Cheese Biscuits *(photo, page 3)*

prep: 10 minutes   cook: 10 minutes

*"Tender," "flaky," and "delicious" were just a few of the enthusiastic
responses to these biscuits, which received our highest test rating.*

2   cups self-rising flour, divided
1   teaspoon sugar
½   cup (4 ounces) ⅓-less-fat cream cheese, cut into small pieces
2   tablespoons chilled reduced-calorie stick margarine
¼   cup plus 3 tablespoons fat-free milk
Cooking spray

Preheat oven to 450°.
Sprinkle 1 tablespoon flour over work surface. Combine remaining
flour and sugar in a bowl; stir well. Cut in cheese with a pastry blender
until mixture resembles coarse meal. Cut in margarine until it forms
small pieces. Add milk, stirring mixture just until dry ingredients
are moist.
Turn dough out onto a lightly floured work surface. Knead 4 or 5
times. Pat dough to ½-inch thickness; cut into rounds with a 2-inch
biscuit cutter. Place rounds on a baking sheet coated with cooking
spray.
Bake at 450° for 10 minutes or until biscuits are lightly browned.
Yield: 14 biscuits (serving size: 1 biscuit).

Per Serving: Calories **97**   Fat **3.2g** (sat **1.4g**)   Protein **2.8g**   Carbohydrate **14.2g**   Fiber **0.0g**
Cholesterol **6mg**   Iron **0.9mg**   Sodium **279mg**   Calcium **76mg**
Exchanges: 1 Starch, ½ Fat

Buttermilk Biscuits

prep: 7 minutes   cook: 10 minutes

For fluffy biscuits, handle dough with a light touch. Take care to keep the cutter straight as you cut the dough so the biscuits will rise evenly.

2   cups all-purpose flour
2½ teaspoons baking powder
¼   teaspoon baking soda
¼   teaspoon salt
2   teaspoons sugar
3   tablespoons chilled reduced-calorie stick margarine, cut into small
       pieces
¾   cup low-fat buttermilk (1%)
Butter-flavored cooking spray

Preheat oven to 425°.
Combine first 5 ingredients in a medium bowl; cut in margarine with a pastry blender until mixture resembles coarse meal. Add buttermilk, stirring just until dry ingredients are moist.
Turn dough out onto a lightly floured surface, and knead 10 to 12 times. Roll dough to ½-inch thickness; cut into rounds with a 2-inch biscuit cutter.
Place rounds on an ungreased baking sheet. Lightly coat biscuits with cooking spray. Bake at 425° for 10 to 12 minutes or until golden.
Yield: 16 biscuits (serving size: 1 biscuit).

Per Serving: Calories **75** Fat **1.6g** (sat **0.1g**) Protein **2.0g** Carbohydrate **13.2g** Fiber **0.4g**
Cholesterol **0mg** Iron **0.8mg** Sodium **167mg** Calcium **59mg**
Exchange: 1 Starch

Cinnamon-Raisin Biscuits

prep: 12 minutes   cook: 10 minutes

A good biscuit dough should be slightly sticky to the touch and should be kneaded gently just a few times.

1¾ cups all-purpose flour
2 . teaspoons baking powder
⅓   cup raisins
2   tablespoons granulated sugar
1¼ teaspoons ground cinnamon
⅔   cup nonfat buttermilk
2   tablespoons vegetable oil
Cooking spray
½   cup sifted powdered sugar
2   tablespoons unsweetened apple juice

Preheat oven to 425°.
Combine first 5 ingredients in a large bowl; make a well in center of mixture. Combine buttermilk and oil; add to flour mixture, stirring just until dry ingredients are moist.
Turn dough out onto a lightly floured work surface; knead 3 to 5 times. Roll dough to ½-inch thickness; cut into rounds with a 2-inch biscuit cutter. Place rounds on a baking sheet coated with cooking spray.
Bake at 425° for 10 minutes or until golden. Combine powdered sugar and apple juice, stirring mixture well; drizzle over warm biscuits.
Yield: 18 biscuits (serving size: 1 biscuit).

Per Serving: Calories 89   Fat **1.7g** (sat **0.3g**)   Protein **1.7g**   Carbohydrate **17.0g**   Fiber **0.5g**
Cholesterol **0mg**   Iron **0.7mg**   Sodium **55mg**   Calcium **46mg**
Exchange: 1 Starch

Buttermilk-Cherry Scones

prep: 12 minutes   cook: 15 minutes

Substitute ⅓ cup chopped dried apricots for the dried cherries for a flavor variation.

2   cups all-purpose flour
1½ teaspoons baking powder
½   teaspoon baking soda
¼   teaspoon salt
¼   cup sugar
¼   cup chilled stick margarine, cut into small pieces
⅔   cup dried tart cherries
1   large egg, lightly beaten
½   cup low-fat buttermilk
Cooking spray
1   large egg white, lightly beaten
1   tablespoon sugar

Preheat oven to 400°.
Combine first 5 ingredients in a bowl; cut in margarine with a pastry blender until mixture resembles coarse meal. Add cherries; toss well. Combine egg and buttermilk; add to dry ingredients, stirring just until moist. (Dough will be sticky.)
Turn dough out onto a lightly floured surface; with floured hands, knead 4 or 5 times. Pat dough into an 8-inch circle on a baking sheet coated with cooking spray. Cut into 12 wedges, cutting to, but not through, bottom of dough. Brush with egg white, and sprinkle with 1 tablespoon sugar. Bake at 400° for 15 minutes or until golden. Serve hot.
Yield: 12 scones (serving size: 1 scone).

Per Serving: Calories **173** Fat **4.5g** (sat **1.0g**) Protein **4.1g** Carbohydrate **28.4g** Fiber **0.9g**
Cholesterol **19mg** Iron **1.2mg** Sodium **239mg** Calcium **69mg**
Exchanges: 2 Starch, 1 Fat

Cranberry Scones

prep: 12 minutes   cook: 20 minutes

Scones are best served right out of the oven. You can enjoy the sweet-tart taste of cranberries in this bread year-round when you use raisin-like dried cranberries.

1½   cups all-purpose flour
½   teaspoon baking soda
¼   teaspoon salt
2   tablespoons sugar
1   teaspoon cream of tartar
3   tablespoons chilled stick margarine, cut into small pieces
⅔   cup sweetened dried cranberries
2   teaspoons grated orange rind
¾   cup nonfat buttermilk
1   tablespoon all-purpose flour
Cooking spray
2   teaspoons sugar

Preheat oven to 375°.
Combine first 5 ingredients in a large bowl; cut in margarine with a pastry blender until mixture resembles coarse meal. Stir in cranberries and orange rind, tossing well. Add buttermilk to dry ingredients, stirring just until dry ingredients are moist.
Sprinkle 1 tablespoon flour evenly over work surface. Turn dough out onto floured surface; with floured hands, knead 4 or 5 times. Divide dough into 2 portions. Pat each portion into a 5-inch circle on a baking sheet coated with cooking spray. Cut each circle into 4 wedges, cutting to, but not through, bottom of dough. Sprinkle each circle evenly with 1 teaspoon sugar. Bake at 375° for 20 minutes or until golden.
Yield: 8 scones (serving size: 1 scone).

Per Serving: Calories 186 Fat **4.6g** (sat **0.9g**) Protein **3.4g** Carbohydrate **32.6g** Fiber **1.2g**
Cholesterol **1mg** Iron **1.3mg** Sodium **228mg** Calcium **34mg**
Exchanges: 1 Starch, 1 Fruit, 1 Fat

Sweet Potato Scones

prep: 12 minutes   cook: 10 minutes

Look for canned whole sweet potatoes in your supermarket. Drain the potatoes, and then mash them to use in this recipe.

1½ cups low-fat baking mix (such as reduced-fat Bisquick)
¼   cup raisins
1   tablespoon sugar
½   teaspoon grated orange rind
½   cup canned mashed sweet potato
¼   cup fat-free milk
½   teaspoon vanilla extract
Cooking spray
1½ teaspoons sugar
⅛   teaspoon ground cinnamon

Preheat oven to 450°.
Combine first 4 ingredients in a large bowl. Combine sweet potato, milk, and vanilla; add to raisin mixture, stirring just until dry ingredients are moist. (Dough will be sticky.)
With floured hands, gather dough into a ball; pat ball into a 7-inch circle on a baking sheet coated with cooking spray.
Cut dough into 8 wedges, cutting to, but not through, bottom of dough. Combine 1½ teaspoons sugar and cinnamon; sprinkle mixture over dough.
Bake at 450° for 10 minutes or until scones are lightly browned.
Yield: 8 scones (serving size: 1 scone).

Per Serving: Calories **138**   Fat **1.6g** (sat **0.3g**)   Protein **2.6g**   Carbohydrate **28.0g**   Fiber **0.7g**
Cholesterol **0mg**   Iron **0.6mg**   Sodium **289mg**   Calcium **25mg**
Exchanges: 2 Starch

Apple Butter-Bran Muffins

prep: 5 minutes   cook: 10 minutes

Apple butter, which has no fat, is actually thick preserves made of apples, sugar, spices, and cider. It adds moisture and sweet apple flavor to these muffins.

1   (7.4-ounce) package honey bran muffin mix
½   cup apple butter
⅓   cup chopped dates
1   tablespoon fat-free milk
1   large egg, lightly beaten
Cooking spray

Preheat oven to 450°.
Combine first 5 ingredients, stirring just until dry ingredients are moist. Spoon batter into muffin cups coated with cooking spray, filling three-fourths full.
Bake at 450° for 10 to 12 minutes or until lightly browned. Remove from pans immediately.
Yield: 8 muffins (serving size: 1 muffin).

Per Serving: Calories **174**   Fat **4.7g** (sat **1.0g**)   Protein **2.5g**   Carbohydrate **31.8g**   Fiber **2.8g**
Cholesterol **28mg**   Iron **0.4mg**   Sodium **212mg**   Calcium **11mg**
Exchanges: 2 Starch, 1 Fat

Lemon-Blueberry Muffins

prep: 12 minutes   cook: 20 minutes

Tangy lemon rind contrasts deliciously with sweet, fresh blueberries in these muffins. Be sure to grate only the yellow part of the rind since the white pith beneath it can be bitter.

2   cups all-purpose flour
1   teaspoon baking powder
½   teaspoon baking soda
½   teaspoon salt
½   cup sugar
1   teaspoon grated lemon rind
¾   cup blueberries
2   large egg whites, lightly beaten
1   (8-ounce) carton lemon fat-free yogurt
½   cup unsweetened applesauce
1   tablespoon vegetable oil
Cooking spray

Preheat oven to 400°.
Combine first 6 ingredients in a large bowl; add blueberries, and toss to coat. Make a well in center of mixture. Combine egg whites and next 3 ingredients; add to dry ingredients, stirring just until dry ingredients are moist.
Spoon batter into muffin cups coated with cooking spray, filling two-thirds full. Bake at 400° for 20 minutes. Remove from pans immediately, and place on a wire rack.
Yield: 16 muffins (serving size: 1 muffin).

Per Serving: Calories **104** Fat **1.2g** (sat **0.2g**) Protein **2.5g** Carbohydrate **20.9g** Fiber **0.8g**
Cholesterol **0mg** Iron **0.7mg** Sodium **115mg** Calcium **29mg**
Exchange: 1 Starch

Pumpkin-Raisin Muffins

prep: 12 minutes   cook: 15 minutes

Pumpkin pie spice is a convenient blend of spices, but you can make your own by combining ³/₄ teaspoon ground cinnamon, ¹/₄ teaspoon ground ginger, and ¹/₈ teaspoon ground nutmeg.

1½ cups all-purpose flour
⅓   cup packed brown sugar
1   teaspoon baking powder
½   teaspoon baking soda
¼   teaspoon salt
1½ teaspoons pumpkin pie spice
⅓   cup raisins
1   large egg, lightly beaten
½   cup canned pumpkin
⅓   cup orange juice
1   tablespoon stick margarine, melted
Cooking spray

Preheat oven to 400°.
Combine first 6 ingredients in a large bowl; stir in raisins. Make a well in center of mixture. Combine egg and next 3 ingredients in a small bowl. Add to dry ingredients, stirring just until dry ingredients are moist. (Batter will be very thick.)
Spoon batter into muffin cups coated with cooking spray, filling two-thirds full. Bake at 400° for 15 minutes. Remove from pans immediately.
Yield: 12 muffins (serving size: 1 muffin).

Per Serving: Calories **116**   Fat **1.8g** (sat **0.4g**)   Protein **2.5g**   Carbohydrate **22.9g**   Fiber **1.1g**
Cholesterol **18mg**   Iron **1.2mg**   Sodium **122mg**   Calcium **39mg**
Exchange: 1 Starch

Corn Bread

prep: 10 minutes   cook: 20 minutes

For a spicy flavor option, add 3 tablespoons minced jalapeño pepper (about 3 small peppers) and ½ cup sliced green onions to the batter.

1¼ cups yellow cornmeal
¾ cup all-purpose flour
2   teaspoons baking powder
½ teaspoon baking soda
¼ teaspoon salt
1   tablespoon sugar
1   cup low-fat buttermilk (1%)
1   (8¾-ounce) can cream-style corn
1   large egg, lightly beaten
Cooking spray

Preheat oven to 425°.
Combine first 6 ingredients in a medium bowl; stir well.
Combine buttermilk, corn, and egg in a small bowl; stir well. Add to cornmeal mixture, stirring just until dry ingredients are moist. Pour batter into an 8-inch square baking pan coated with cooking spray.
Bake at 425° for 20 to 22 minutes or until golden. Cool 5 minutes in pan on a wire rack. Remove from pan, and cut into squares. Serve warm.
Yield: 9 servings (serving size: 1 square).

Per Serving: Calories **145** Fat **1.6g** (sat **0.4g**) Protein **4.6g** Carbohydrate **28.6g** Fiber **2.6g**
Cholesterol **25mg** Iron **1.4mg** Sodium **367mg** Calcium **99mg**
Exchanges: 2 Starch

Chipotle Chile Corn Bread *(photo, page 2)*

prep: 6 minutes   cook: 23 minutes

You can use an eight-inch square pan instead of an eight-inch cast iron skillet. Serve this spicy corn bread with your favorite soup or chili.

Cooking spray
2   cups self-rising buttermilk cornmeal mix
1   cup nonfat buttermilk
2   tablespoons vegetable oil
1   to 2 tablespoons chopped chipotle chile in adobo sauce
        (or ¼ teaspoon ground red pepper)
2   teaspoons sugar
1   large egg, lightly beaten

Preheat oven to 425°.
Coat an 8-inch cast iron skillet with cooking spray; place in preheated oven 5 minutes or until hot.
Combine cornmeal mix and remaining 5 ingredients in a large bowl, stirring just until dry ingredients are moist. Pour batter into hot skillet. Bake at 425° for 23 to 25 minutes or until corn bread is golden.
Yield: 8 servings (serving size: 1 slice).

Per Serving: Calories **159** Fat **5.3g** (sat **1.1g**) Protein **4.5g** Carbohydrate **24.4g** Fiber **0.2g**
Cholesterol **29mg** Iron **1.9mg** Sodium **446mg** Calcium **151mg**
Exchanges: 1½ Starch, 1 Fat

Corn Muffins

prep: 8 minutes   cook: 20 minutes

Try this quick way to mince green onions: Hold several onions together in one hand while you snip them with kitchen shears.

2½ cups self-rising flour
3   tablespoons minced green onions (about 2)
½   cup fat-free milk
½   cup egg substitute
1½ tablespoons vegetable oil
1   (8¾-ounce) can no-salt-added cream-style corn
Cooking spray

Preheat oven to 400°.
Combine flour and green onions in a medium bowl; make a well in center of mixture. Combine milk and next 3 ingredients; add to dry ingredients, stirring just until dry ingredients are moist.
Spoon batter into muffin cups coated with cooking spray, filling two-thirds full. Bake at 400° for 20 minutes. Remove from pans immediately, and serve warm.
Yield: 12 muffins (serving size: 1 muffin).

Per Serving: Calories **132**   Fat **2.3g** (sat **0.4g**)   Protein **4.3g**   Carbohydrate **23.5g**   Fiber **1.1g**
Cholesterol **0mg**   Iron **1.5mg**   Sodium **352mg**   Calcium **105mg**
Exchange: 1 Starch

Corn Sticks

prep: 9 minutes   cook: 10 minutes

A preheated cast iron pan gives corn bread a crunchy, browned crust. The batter crisps quickly in the hot pan while the inside of the bread bakes slowly and stays moist.

¾ cup all-purpose flour
¾ cup yellow cornmeal
2   teaspoons baking powder
¼ teaspoon baking soda
¼ teaspoon salt
1½ tablespoons sugar
⅛ teaspoon ground red pepper
1   (6½-ounce) can whole-kernel corn, drained
1   large egg, lightly beaten
1   cup nonfat buttermilk
Cooking spray

Preheat oven to 425°.
Combine first 7 ingredients in a medium bowl. Add corn, stirring well; make a well in center of mixture. Combine egg and buttermilk; add to flour mixture, stirring just until moist.
Place cast iron corn stick pans in oven 5 minutes or until hot. Remove pans from oven, and coat with cooking spray. Spoon batter evenly into pans. Bake at 425° for 10 minutes or until lightly browned. Remove corn sticks from pans immediately, and serve warm.
Yield: 14 corn sticks (serving size: 1 corn stick).

Per Serving: Calories **83** Fat **0.9g** (sat **0.2g**) Protein **2.8g** Carbohydrate **16.3g** Fiber **0.7g**
Cholesterol **16mg** Iron **0.8mg** Sodium **113mg** Calcium **51mg**
Exchange: 1 Starch

desserts

• make ahead •

Stirred Vanilla Custard

prep: 5 minutes   cook: 10 minutes

This creamy custard has a consistency similar to eggnog. Spoon it over fresh melon or mixed berries for a special dessert.

3   cups fat-free milk
2   large eggs
½   cup sugar
1½ tablespoons all-purpose flour
⅛   teaspoon salt
1   teaspoon vanilla extract
Ground nutmeg (optional)

Heat milk in a heavy saucepan over low heat until very hot, stirring occasionally (do not boil).
While milk heats, beat eggs with a mixer at medium speed until foamy. Add sugar, flour, and salt, beating until thick. Gradually stir about 1 cup hot milk into egg mixture; add to remaining hot mixture, stirring constantly.
Cook, stirring constantly, over medium heat 7 minutes or until thickened. Remove from heat, and stir in vanilla. Spoon ½ cup custard into each of 6 dessert bowls. Sprinkle ground nutmeg lightly over each serving, if desired. Serve custard warm or chilled.
Yield: 6 servings.

Per Serving: Calories **141**   Fat **2.0g** (sat **0.7g**)   Protein **6.4g**   Carbohydrate **24.2g**   Fiber **0.1g**
Cholesterol **76mg**   Iron **0.4mg**   Sodium **132mg**   Calcium **155mg**
Exchanges: 1½ Starch, ½ Fat

Double-Chocolate Banana Pudding

prep: 15 minutes

Here's a chocolate twist on an American tradition. If you love chocolate AND bananas, you're in for a real treat with this unique pudding combo.

2   (3.4-ounce) packages white chocolate instant pudding mix
3½ cups fat-free milk
1   (8-ounce) carton fat-free sour cream
1   teaspoon vanilla extract
2   cups frozen reduced-calorie whipped topping, thawed
62 reduced-fat chocolate wafer cookies
3   large bananas, peeled

Combine first 4 ingredients in a large bowl; beat with a mixer at low speed 3 minutes or until thickened. Fold in whipped topping.
Line bottom of a 3-quart bowl with chocolate wafer cookies. Slice 1 banana, and layer slices over wafers. Spoon one-third of pudding mixture over banana. Repeat layers twice.
Place remaining chocolate wafers around top edge of dessert. Serve immediately, or cover and chill until ready to serve.
Yield: 14 servings.

Per Serving: Calories **175**   Fat **3.4g** (sat **1.6g**)   Protein **4.3g**   Carbohydrate **32.7g**   Fiber **0.7g**
Cholesterol **1mg**   Iron **0.2mg**   Sodium **244mg**   Calcium **85mg**
Exchanges: 2 Starch, ½ Fat

Black Forest Parfaits *(photo, back cover)*

prep: 8 minutes

Layers of rich white chocolate pudding and sweet cherries give this dessert an elegant appearance for company, yet it's quick enough to prepare on the spur of the moment for family. You can serve the parfaits right after you make them, but it's okay to chill them for later, too.

1   (3.4-ounce) package white chocolate instant pudding mix
2   cups fat-free milk
1   (20-ounce) can light cherry pie filling
¾   cup chocolate wafer cookie crumbs (about 16 cookies)
¼   cup plus 2 tablespoons frozen reduced-calorie whipped topping,
        thawed
Cherries (optional)

Prepare pudding mix according to package directions, using 2 cups fat-free milk.
Divide half of pudding evenly among 6 (6-ounce) parfait or stemmed glasses. Spoon half of pie filling evenly over pudding in glasses.
Top parfaits evenly with half of cookie crumbs. Repeat layers with remaining pudding, pie filling, and cookie crumbs. Top each serving with 1 tablespoon whipped topping, and garnish with fresh cherries, if desired.
Yield: 6 servings.

Per Serving: Calories 195   Fat **1.8g** (sat **0.4g**)   Protein **4.3g**   Carbohydrate **41.3g**   Fiber **0.8g**
Cholesterol **2mg**   Iron **0.6mg**   Sodium **335mg**   Calcium **127mg**
Exchanges: 2 Starch, 1 Fruit

Double Berry-Brownie Dessert

prep: 10 minutes

If you've recently made a batch of brownies from a low-fat brownie mix, here's a great recipe for finishing off any leftovers. Strawberries and raspberries add a fancy touch to the brownies, but it's the whipped topping and the hot fudge that truly make this dessert doubly delicious.

3   tablespoons seedless strawberry jam, melted
1½ tablespoons water
1   cup raspberries
1   cup sliced strawberries
4   low-fat chocolate brownies
¾   cup frozen fat-free whipped topping, thawed
¼   cup fat-free hot fudge topping

Combine jam and water in a medium bowl; stir in raspberries and strawberries. Reserve 2 tablespoons berry mixture for topping. Tear brownies into small pieces, reserving several pieces for topping.
Place several brownie pieces in each of 4 dessert cups. Spoon about ¼ cup berry mixture over brownie. Repeat layers. Top each with whipped topping, fudge topping, reserved berry mixture, and reserved brownie pieces.

Yield: 4 servings (serving size: 1 brownie, ½ cup berry mixture, 3 tablespoons whipped topping, and 1 tablespoon fudge topping).

Per Serving: Calories **268**   Fat **2.8g** (sat **1.0g**)   Protein **1.5g**   Carbohydrate **59.7g**   Fiber **4.0g**
Cholesterol **0mg**   Iron **1.6mg**   Sodium **141mg**   Calcium **23mg**
Exchanges: 3 Starch, 1 Fruit, ½ Fat

Chocolate-Glazed Coconut Cream Cake

prep: 15 minutes

For a warm glaze, heat the frosting and milk mixture in the microwave at HIGH for 20 seconds.

1   (3.4-ounce) package coconut cream instant pudding mix
1¾ cups fat-free milk
¼   cup reduced-fat milk chocolate-flavored frosting (such as Sweet
        Rewards)
2   teaspoons fat-free milk
1   (13.6-ounce) fat-free golden loaf (such as Entenmann's)

Prepare pudding mix according to package directions, using 1¾ cups fat-free milk. Cover and chill 5 minutes.

Combine frosting and milk in a small bowl, stirring well. Set aside.

Slice cake horizontally into 4 layers, using a sharp serrated knife or an electric knife. Spoon ⅓ cup pudding on bottom layer. Top with a layer of cake. Repeat procedure twice, ending with top cake layer. (Reserve remaining pudding for another use.) Pour glaze over cake. Slice with a sharp serrated knife or an electric knife.

Yield: 10 servings (serving size: 1 slice).

Per Serving: Calories **184**   Fat **1.6g** (sat **1.3g**)   Protein **3.1g**   Carbohydrate **37.7g**   Fiber **0.0g**
Cholesterol **2mg**   Iron **0.0mg**   Sodium **287mg**   Calcium **54mg**
Exchanges: 2½ Starch

Chocolate-Almond Fondue

prep: 11 minutes

To serve a traditional fondue dessert, keep the sauce warm in a fondue pot or chafing dish. Let guests dip strawberries and cake into the warm sauce with fondue sticks or wooden picks. Or use the sauce to top ice cream or to drizzle over cake or fruit. The recipe makes 1½ cups of sauce.

1   (14-ounce) can fat-free sweetened condensed milk
½   cup reduced-fat semisweet chocolate baking chips
½   teaspoon almond extract
24   strawberries
24   (1-inch) cubes angel food cake (about ¼ of 16-ounce cake)

Combine milk and chocolate in a medium saucepan over low heat. Cook, stirring constantly, about 3 minutes or until chocolate melts. Remove from heat, and stir in almond extract. Serve warm with strawberries and cake.

Yield: 24 servings (serving size: 1 tablespoon sauce, 1 strawberry, and 1 cake cube).

Per Serving: Calories **81**   Fat **1.2g** (sat **1.2g**)   Protein **0.5g**   Carbohydrate **17.1g**   Fiber **0.4g**
Cholesterol **0mg**   Iron **0.1mg**   Sodium **38mg**   Calcium **6mg**
Exchange: 1 Starch

Caramel-Apple Cake *(photo, page 15)*

prep: 7 minutes   cook: 27 minutes

To toast pecans, place pecans in a hot small nonstick skillet (no oil needed) over medium heat; cook, stirring constantly, for 2 to 3 minutes. You'll be amazed how toasting enhances the rich flavor of the nuts.

2   (7-ounce) packages apple-cinnamon muffin mix
1   cup fat-free milk
2   large egg whites
3   tablespoons reduced-fat sour cream
2½ tablespoons fat-free caramel topping
3   tablespoons chopped pecans, toasted

Preheat oven to 375°.

Prepare muffin mix according to package directions, using 1 cup milk and egg whites. Pour batter into an 8-inch square pan. Bake at 375° for 27 minutes or until lightly browned.

While cake bakes, combine sour cream and caramel topping, stirring until frosting is smooth.

Spread frosting over warm cake, and sprinkle with toasted pecans. Serve warm.

Yield: 9 servings (serving size: 1 square).

Per Serving: Calories **230**   Fat **6.3g** (sat **1.7g**)   Protein **4.6g**   Carbohydrate **37.8g**   Fiber **0.8g**
Cholesterol **3mg**   Iron **1.3mg**   Sodium **416mg**   Calcium **49mg**
Exchanges: 2½ Starch, 1 Fat

Caramelized Orange Bananas

prep: 12 minutes

Here's a rich-tasting dessert that will remind you of Bananas Foster. This nonalcoholic version doesn't require flaming.

2	large bananas, peeled
1½	teaspoons reduced-calorie stick margarine
¼	cup packed brown sugar
¼	cup unsweetened orange juice
⅛	to ¼ teaspoon banana extract
2	cups vanilla fat-free ice cream

Cut each banana in half. Cut banana halves lengthwise into quarters; set aside.

Add margarine to a medium skillet, and place over medium heat until margarine melts. Stir in brown sugar, and cook, stirring constantly, until sugar dissolves and mixture begins to bubble. Stir in orange juice, and add bananas to pan. Increase heat to medium-high, and cook 2 minutes, stirring gently. Turn bananas, and sprinkle with banana extract.

Spoon ½ cup ice cream into each of 4 dessert bowls; spoon warm bananas evenly over ice cream. Serve immediately.

Yield: 4 servings.

Per Serving: Calories **199** Fat **1.2g** (sat **0.1g**) Protein **2.7g** Carbohydrate **45.1g** Fiber **1.6g**
Cholesterol **0mg** Iron **0.4mg** Sodium **58mg** Calcium **12mg**
Exchanges: 1 Starch, 2 Fruit

Caramel-Toffee Parfaits

prep: 12 minutes

For a no-mess way to crush the candy bar, place it in a zip-top plastic bag, seal the bag, and crush it with a rolling pin.

1   large banana, peeled
2   cups vanilla fat-free ice cream
2   tablespoons plus 2 teaspoons fat-free caramel or chocolate topping
1   (1.4-ounce) chocolate toffee crisp bar, finely crushed (such as
        HEATH Milk Chocolate English Toffee Bar)

Cut banana in half crosswise. Cut each banana half in half lengthwise. Place 1 banana piece in each of 4 (4-ounce) parfait glasses.

Spoon ¼ cup ice cream into the bottom of each parfait glass; top each with 1 teaspoon caramel topping. Sprinkle half of crushed candy evenly over parfaits. Repeat layers. Serve immediately.

Yield: 4 servings.

Per Serving: Calories **226**   Fat **2.2g** (sat **1.3g**)   Protein **4.1g**   Carbohydrate **48.9g**   Fiber **0.9g**
Cholesterol **0mg**   Iron **0.1mg**   Sodium **109mg**   Calcium **2mg**
Exchanges: 2 Starch, 1 Fruit, ½ Fat

Island Fruit Dessert

prep: 10 minutes

To toast the coconut, spread it in a thin layer in the bottom of a pie plate, and microwave at HIGH 1 to 2 minutes, stirring every 30 seconds.

2   (8-ounce) cartons vanilla low-fat yogurt
1   cup halved seedless red grapes
1   medium banana, peeled and sliced
1   (8.25-ounce) can apricot halves in extralight syrup, drained and
        sliced
1   (8-ounce) can pineapple chunks in juice, drained
2   tablespoons apricot spread (such as Polaner All Fruit)
¼   cup flaked coconut, toasted

Spoon yogurt onto several layers of heavy-duty paper towels; spread to ½-inch thickness. Cover with additional paper towels; let stand 5 minutes.

While yogurt stands, combine grapes and next 3 ingredients in a bowl; spoon evenly into each of 4 dessert dishes.

Scrape yogurt from paper towels into a small bowl, using a rubber spatula. Stir apricot spread into yogurt; spoon yogurt mixture evenly over fruit. Sprinkle evenly with coconut.

Yield: 4 servings (serving size: ¾ cup).

Per Serving: Calories **190**   Fat **3.1g** (sat **2.4g**)   Protein **3.7g**   Carbohydrate **36.7g**   Fiber **2.2g**
Cholesterol **3mg**   Iron **0.6mg**   Sodium **57mg**   Calcium **110mg**
Exchanges: 1 Starch, 1½ Fruit, ½ Fat

Mixed Berry Dessert

prep: 4 minutes

For a nonalcoholic version, use orange juice instead of the Grand Marnier.

3 tablespoons Grand Marnier or other orange-flavored liqueur
½ teaspoon grated orange rind
1 tablespoon sugar
1 cup blueberries
1 cup blackberries or raspberries
½ cup frozen fat-free whipped topping, thawed
Orange curls or grated orange rind (optional)

Combine first 3 ingredients in a medium bowl, stirring until sugar dissolves. Add blueberries and blackberries, tossing gently.
Spoon ½ cup mixture into each of 4 dessert dishes. Top each serving with 2 tablespoons whipped topping. If desired, garnish with orange curls or orange rind.
Yield: 4 servings.

Per Serving: Calories **106**   Fat **0.3g** (sat **0.0g**)   Protein **0.5g**   Carbohydrate **20.0g**   Fiber **4.6g**
Cholesterol **0mg**   Iron **0.3mg**   Sodium **8mg**   Calcium **15mg**
Exchange: 1 Fruit

Lemon Sorbet with Tropical Fruit Sauce

prep: 12 minutes

Kiwifruit tastes like a blend of strawberry and banana. If you can't find kiwifruit, substitute 1 small banana, sliced, and 6 sliced fresh strawberries.

1   (11-ounce) can mandarin oranges in light syrup, undrained
1   teaspoon cornstarch
2   sliced peeled kiwifruit
3   cups lemon fat-free sorbet or fat-free ice cream

Drain oranges, reserving juice; set oranges aside.
Combine juice and cornstarch in a small saucepan over medium-high heat. Bring to a boil; reduce heat to medium, and cook 1 minute or until thickened. Place saucepan in a bowl of ice; let stand 5 minutes or until cool, stirring often. Stir in oranges and kiwifruit.
Spoon ½ cup sorbet into each of 6 dessert bowls. Spoon fruit sauce evenly over sorbet.
Yield: 6 servings.

Per Serving: Calories **191** Fat **0.2g** (sat **0.0g**) Protein **0.4g** Carbohydrate **47.9g** Fiber **0.9g**
Cholesterol **0mg** Iron **0.2mg** Sodium **3mg** Calcium **7mg**
Exchanges: 3 Fruit

Lemon-Raspberry Tarts *(photo, page 12)*

prep: 10 minutes

You can make these tarts at least 3 hours ahead, and store them in the refrigerator. It's not necessary to thaw the phyllo shells before filling them.

1   tablespoon plus 1 teaspoon raspberry spread (such as Polaner All Fruit)
1   (2.1-ounce) package frozen miniature phyllo shells
¼   cup plus 1 tablespoon lemon curd
½   cup frozen fat-free whipped topping, thawed
15   raspberries
Mint sprigs (optional)

Spoon ¼ teaspoon raspberry spread into the bottom of each frozen phyllo shell. Spoon 1 teaspoon lemon curd over raspberry spread in each shell. Spoon whipped topping evenly over lemon curd.
Place 1 raspberry on each tart. Garnish with mint, if desired.
Yield: 15 tarts (serving size: 1 tart).

Per Serving: Calories **48** Fat **0.1g** (sat **0.0g**) Protein **0.5g** Carbohydrate **8.0g** Fiber **0.2g**
Cholesterol **0mg** Iron **0.0mg** Sodium **11mg** Calcium **1mg**
Exchange: ½ Starch

Citrusy Melon and Strawberry Cup

prep: 5 minutes

This simple dessert shows off several of the most nutrient-packed fruits. Cantaloupe is the most nutritious of all melons, while a cup of strawberries has more fiber than a slice of whole wheat bread. Keep prep time to a minimum by picking up precut fruit from your grocer's produce or deli department.

1   tablespoon sugar
1   tablespoon lemon juice
3   tablespoons frozen orange juice concentrate, thawed
1½ cups bite-sized cantaloupe chunks
1½ cups bite-sized honeydew melon chunks
1   cup halved strawberries

Combine first 3 ingredients in a large bowl; stir well. Add remaining ingredients; stir gently.

Spoon 1 cup fruit mixture into each of 4 dessert cups.

Yield: 4 servings.

Per Serving: Calories **86** Fat **0.4g** (sat **0.1g**) Protein **1.3g** Carbohydrate **21.2g** Fiber **1.8g** Cholesterol **0mg** Iron **0.4mg** Sodium **11mg** Calcium **20mg**
Exchanges: 1½ Fruit

Blueberry Sauce

cook: 8 minutes

This versatile blueberry sauce tastes yummy over waffles, angel food cake, or pancakes, too.

3   tablespoons sugar
1½   teaspoons cornstarch
½   cup water
1   cup blueberries

Combine sugar and cornstarch in a small saucepan; gradually stir in water. Bring mixture to a boil over medium-high heat, stirring constantly. Add blueberries, and cook 4 minutes or until mixture boils in center, stirring often. Reduce heat to medium, and cook 2 minutes, stirring often; cool slightly.
Yield: 1 cup (serving size: ¼ cup).

Per Serving: Calories **60**   Fat **0.1g** (sat **0.0g**)   Protein **0.3g**   Carbohydrate **15.4g**   Fiber **1.0g**
Cholesterol **0mg**   Iron **0.1mg**   Sodium **2mg**   Calcium **2.3mg**
Exchange: 1 Fruit

Peach Sundaes with Blueberry Sauce

prep: 13 minutes

Blueberry Sauce (recipe above)
1   cup cubed peeled peaches (about 2)
1⅓   cups vanilla low-fat ice cream

Prepare Blueberry Sauce.
Place ¼ cup peaches in each of 4 dessert dishes; top each with ⅓ cup ice cream and ¼ cup Blueberry Sauce. Serve immediately.
Yield: 4 servings.

Per Serving: Calories **145**   Fat **1.5g** (sat **1.0g**)   Protein **2.5g**   Carbohydrate **32.0g**   Fiber **2.5g**
Cholesterol **7mg**   Iron **0.1mg**   Sodium **6mg**   Calcium **71mg**
Exchanges: 1½ Starch, 1½ Fruit

Peach Melba Brûlée *(photo, page 13)*

prep: 16 minutes

A brûlée (French for "burned") is a dessert featuring sugar that has been caramelized at high heat. If you don't have dishes that are safe for the broiler, bake the brûlée at 400° for 10 minutes for a "melted" sugar dessert.

1   (29-ounce) can sliced peaches in extralight syrup, undrained
3   ounces angel food cake, cut into ½-inch cubes (about 2 cups)
¼   cup seedless raspberry spread (such as Polaner All Fruit)
¾   cup low-fat sour cream
¼   cup plus 2 tablespoons brown sugar

Preheat broiler.
Drain peaches, reserving 1 tablespoon syrup; pat peaches dry with paper towels. Set aside.
Divide cake cubes evenly among 6 (8-ounce) ramekins or custard cups. Combine raspberry spread and reserved peach syrup; stir until smooth. Spoon 2 teaspoons raspberry mixture over cake in each dish. Spoon peaches evenly over raspberry mixture; top each serving with 2 tablespoons sour cream. Sprinkle each with 1 tablespoon brown sugar.
Place ramekins on a baking sheet. Broil 3 minutes or until sugar melts and begins to bubble. Serve immediately.
Yield: 6 servings.

Per Serving: Calories **205**   Fat **3.6g** (sat **2.2g**)   Protein **1.7g**   Carbohydrate **42.2g**   Fiber **0.8g**
Cholesterol **11mg**   Iron **0.3mg**   Sodium **98mg**   Calcium **55mg**
Exchanges: 1 Starch, 2 Fruit, 1 Fat

Peach Shortcakes

prep: 14 minutes

To thaw a carton of whipped topping, remove the lid, and heat in the microwave at MEDIUM-LOW (30% power) for 1 to 2 minutes. After thawing, whipped topping will keep for about two weeks in the refrigerator.

1   cup plus 2 tablespoons low-fat baking mix (such as reduced-fat Bisquick)
3   tablespoons sugar, divided
⅛   teaspoon ground cinnamon
⅛   teaspoon ground nutmeg
⅓   cup low-fat milk
1   tablespoon stick margarine, melted
2   cups frozen sliced peaches
¼   cup frozen fat-free whipped topping, thawed

Preheat oven to 425°.

Combine baking mix, 2 tablespoons sugar, cinnamon, and nutmeg; stir well. Add milk and margarine, stirring just until combined.

Drop dough by spoonfuls onto an ungreased baking sheet, spreading each mound to a 3-inch circle. Bake at 425° for 7 minutes or until golden.

While shortcakes bake, place peaches in a microwave-safe bowl. Microwave at MEDIUM-LOW (30% power) 5 to 6 minutes or until thawed. Use a fork to break apart peaches. Sprinkle peaches with remaining 1 tablespoon sugar; stir well.

Split each shortcake in half horizontally. Place bottom halves of cakes on each of 4 dessert plates. Top each with ½ cup peach mixture. Arrange remaining cake halves over peaches. Top each with 1 tablespoon whipped topping. Serve warm.

Yield: 4 servings.

Per Serving: Calories **240**   Fat **5.2g** (sat **1.1g**)   Protein **3.8g**   Carbohydrate **44.6g**   Fiber **1.3g**
Cholesterol **1mg**   Iron **0.1mg**   Sodium **434mg**   Calcium **31mg**
Exchanges: 1 Starch, 2 Fruit, 1 Fat

Summer Fruit Crisp

prep: 15 minutes   cook: 40 minutes

Juicy summer peaches and blueberries taste even sweeter with a cinnamon-scented topping of oats and brown sugar.

¼   cup granulated sugar
3   tablespoons all-purpose flour
1   teaspoon grated lemon rind
3   cups sliced peaches
2   cups blueberries
Cooking spray
¾   cup regular oats, uncooked
⅓   cup packed brown sugar
3   tablespoons whole wheat flour
2   teaspoons ground cinnamon
3   tablespoons reduced-calorie stick margarine, chilled and cut into
        small pieces

Preheat oven to 375°.
Combine first 3 ingredients in a medium bowl; stir well. Add peaches and blueberries; toss gently. Spoon mixture into an 8-inch square baking dish coated with cooking spray.
Combine oats and next 3 ingredients in a small bowl; cut in margarine with a pastry blender until mixture is crumbly. Sprinkle over fruit mixture. Bake at 375° for 40 to 45 minutes or until topping is lightly browned.
Yield: 8 servings (serving size: about ¾ cup).

Per Serving: Calories **209**   Fat **2.9g** (sat **0.3g**)   Protein **2.3g**   Carbohydrate **46.2g**   Fiber **2.6g**
Cholesterol **0mg**   Iron **1.2mg**   Sodium **45mg**   Calcium **130mg**
Exchanges: 2 Starch, 1 Fruit

Peach Ice Cream

prep: 12 minutes

Use orange juice concentrate to add a bright, citrusy flavor. It's not necessary to thaw the concentrate for this recipe. Simply spoon the amount you need into a measuring cup. Tightly cover the remaining concentrate, and return to the freezer.

1   (1-pound) package frozen peaches
1½ cups sliced ripe banana (about 2 medium)
1   cup low-fat vanilla ice cream
½   cup frozen orange juice concentrate
¼   cup sifted powdered sugar
¾   to 1 teaspoon coconut extract

Place all ingredients in a food processor; process until smooth. Serve immediately, or freeze, covered, in an airtight freezer-safe container until ready to serve.

Yield: 6 servings (serving size: ¾ cup).

Per Serving: Calories **160**   Fat **0.9g** (sat **0.6g**)   Protein **2.5g**   Carbohydrate **37.0g**   Fiber **2.6g**
Cholesterol **3mg**   Iron **0.2mg**   Sodium **3mg**   Calcium **44mg**
Exchanges: 1 Starch, 1½ Fruit

Rum-Glazed Pineapple

prep: 8 minutes

With one recipe you get two payoffs: 1) it's easy to double to serve a crowd, and 2) it's saucy enough to serve over angel food cake.

1	(20-ounce) can pineapple chunks in juice, undrained
2	teaspoons stick margarine
3	tablespoons brown sugar
2	tablespoons dark rum
1/4	teaspoon cornstarch
2	tablespoons flaked coconut, toasted

Drain pineapple, reserving 1/3 cup juice.
Melt margarine in a large nonstick skillet over medium-high heat. Add pineapple juice, brown sugar, and pineapple chunks, stirring well. Bring to a boil; reduce heat, and simmer 2 to 3 minutes, stirring often.
Combine rum and cornstarch, stirring well; add to pan. Cook 1 minute or until slightly thickened.
Spoon pineapple mixture into a serving dish; sprinkle with coconut. Serve warm.
Yield: 4 servings (serving size: 1/2 cup).

Per Serving: Calories **134** Fat **3.1g** (sat **1.4g**) Protein **0.6g** Carbohydrate **27.5g** Fiber **0.5g**
Cholesterol **0mg** Iron **0.7mg** Sodium **35mg** Calcium **28mg**
Exchanges: 2 Fruit, 1/2 Fat

Pineapple-Mint Ice

prep: 3 minutes   freeze: 2 hours

Need an easy way to get in your five fruit or vegetable servings a day? One serving of this frozen delight counts as two fruits. You can substitute any canned fruit packed in its own juice. You'll be amazed that something so simple to prepare can be so refreshing.

1   (20-ounce) can pineapple chunks in juice, chilled and undrained
2   tablespoons coarsely chopped fresh mint
Mint sprigs (optional)

Set aside 3 pineapple chunks for garnish. Place remaining pineapple and juice into an 8-inch square pan. Cover and freeze 1½ to 2 hours or until almost frozen.

Place frozen pineapple and chopped mint in a food processor; process until smooth, but not melted. Serve immediately; garnish with reserved pineapple chunks and mint sprigs, if desired.

Yield: 3 servings (serving size: ¾ cup).

Per Serving: Calories **117**   Fat **0.0g** (sat **0.0g**)   Protein **0.0g**   Carbohydrate **28.9g**   Fiber **1.4g**   Cholesterol **0mg**   Iron **0.6mg**   Sodium **2mg**   Calcium **20mg**
Exchanges: 2 Fruit

Fresh Strawberries with Lime Custard *(photo, page 15)*

prep: 15 minutes

Substitute your favorite berry in this dessert. Use lemon or orange rind and juice instead of lime rind and juice, if desired. It's easier to grate the rind before squeezing the juice from a lemon, lime, or orange.

1   (8-ounce) carton fat-free sour cream
½   cup fat-free sweetened condensed milk
½   teaspoon grated lime rind
1½ tablespoons fresh lime juice (about 1 medium lime)
3   cups sliced strawberries
Lime rind curls (optional)

Combine first 4 ingredients, stirring well.
Spoon ¼ cup lime custard into each of 4 (6-ounce) custard cups or dessert dishes. Top each with ¾ cup strawberries. Top each serving with 2 tablespoons lime custard. Garnish with lime rind curls, if desired.
Yield: 4 servings.

Per Serving: Calories 190   Fat **0.5g** (sat **0.0g**)   Protein **7.8g**   Carbohydrate **37.5g**   Fiber **3.3g**
Cholesterol **5mg**   Iron **0.5mg**   Sodium **81mg**   Calcium **119mg**
Exchanges: 1 Starch, 1½ Fruit

Orange-Strawberry Trifle

prep: 15 minutes

Substitute mandarin orange syrup from the can or orange juice for the Grand Marnier for a nonalcoholic version.

3   (8-ounce) cartons orange cream low-fat yogurt
1   (8-ounce) carton fat-free sour cream
2   (11-ounce) cans mandarin oranges in light syrup, undrained
1   tablespoon Grand Marnier or other orange-flavored liqueur
8   ounces angel food cake, cut into ¾-inch cubes (about 5 cups)
4   cups strawberries, halved
Mint sprig (optional)

Combine yogurt and sour cream; set aside.
Drain oranges, reserving 3 tablespoons syrup. Set aside oranges. Combine syrup and liqueur.
Arrange half of cake cubes in a 2-quart trifle bowl. Pour half of syrup mixture evenly over cake cubes. Top with half of yogurt mixture. Arrange half of oranges and strawberries over yogurt. Repeat procedure with remaining cake, syrup mixture, yogurt mixture, and fruit. Serve immediately or chill up to 3 hours. Just before serving, garnish with mint, if desired.

Yield: 8 servings (serving size: about 1 cup).

Per Serving: Calories **237**   Fat **1.1g** (sat **0.4g**)   Protein **7.5g**   Carbohydrate **48.8g**   Fiber **1.7g**   Cholesterol **8mg**   Iron **0.4mg**   Sodium **215mg**   Calcium **33mg**
Exchanges: 2½ Starch, 1 Fruit

Gingersnap-Date Balls

prep: 15 minutes

You can use a plastic bag and a rolling pin instead of the food processor to crush the cookies. Here's how: Place the cookies in a large heavy-duty, zip-top plastic bag. Remove the air from the bag, and seal securely. Finely crush the cookies, using a rolling pin or meat mallet. Finely chop the dates and pecans; combine with the cookie crumbs in a bowl. Add the orange juice concentrate and honey, stirring until the dry ingredients are evenly moistened. Continue with the directions in the method.

38   reduced-fat gingersnap cookies
¼   cup chopped dates
¼   cup chopped pecans
3   tablespoons frozen orange juice concentrate, thawed and
        undiluted
2   tablespoons honey
¼   cup sifted powdered sugar

Place cookies in a food processor; pulse 15 times or until cookies are finely ground. Add dates and pecans; pulse 12 times or until finely chopped. Add orange juice concentrate and honey; pulse 8 times or until mixture is evenly moistened.

Shape mixture into 1-inch balls. Roll balls in powdered sugar. Store in an airtight container in refrigerator.

Yield: 24 balls (serving size: 1 ball).

Per Serving: Calories **68** Fat **2.0g** (sat **0.4g**) Protein **0.5g** Carbohydrate **12.4g** Fiber **0.3g**
Cholesterol **0mg** Iron **0.1mg** Sodium **41mg** Calcium **2mg**
Exchange: 1 Fruit

Fudgy Mint Brownie Bites

prep: 12 minutes   cook: 16 minutes

If you prefer the pan method for preparing brownies instead of the muffin method, follow the directions below.

1   (20.5-ounce) package low-fat fudge brownie mix
⅓   cup semisweet chocolate minichips
½   cup water
½   teaspoon peppermint extract
Cooking spray

Preheat oven to 350°.
Combine brownie mix and minichips in a large bowl. Combine water and extract. Add liquid to brownie mix, stirring well.
Spoon 1 tablespoon batter into each of 30 miniature muffin cups heavily coated with cooking spray. Bake at 350° for 16 minutes. Cool completely in pans.
Yield: 30 brownie bites (serving size: 1 brownie bite).

Per Serving: Calories **91** Fat **2.4g** (sat **1.0g**) Protein **1.3g** Carbohydrate **17.6g** Fiber **0.7g** Cholesterol **0mg** Iron **0.7mg** Sodium **70mg** Calcium **1mg**
Exchange: 1 Starch

Pan Brownies

Prepare batter as directed above; spoon into a 13 x 9-inch pan heavily coated with cooking spray. Bake at 350° for 25 to 27 minutes. Place on a wire rack, and cool completely.
Yield: 24 brownies (serving size: 1 brownie).

Per Serving: Calories **113** Fat **2.9g** (sat **1.2g**) Protein **1.6g** Carbohydrate **22.0g** Fiber **0.9g** Cholesterol **0mg** Iron **0.9mg** Sodium **87mg** Calcium **1mg**
Exchange: 1 Starch, ½ Fat

Crispy Cocoa-Cranberry Bars

prep: 10 minutes

Coat the spoon with cooking spray before you stir the cereal into the marshmallow mixture; this will keep the cereal from sticking to the spoon.

1   (10-ounce) package large marshmallows
2   tablespoons stick margarine
6   cups chocolate-flavored oven-toasted rice cereal (such as Rice Krispies)
1   cup sweetened dried cranberries or raisins
½   cup miniature semisweet chocolate chips
Cooking spray

Combine marshmallows and margarine in a large microwave-safe bowl. Microwave at HIGH 2 minutes. Stir well, and microwave 1 additional minute.

While marshmallow mixture heats, combine cereal, cranberries, and chocolate chips in a large bowl. Pour marshmallow mixture over cereal mixture, stirring until well combined.

Press cereal mixture into a 13 x 9-inch baking dish coated with cooking spray. Let cool completely; cut into bars.

Yield: 24 bars (serving size: 1 bar).

Per Serving: Calories **121**   Fat **2.8g** (sat **1.2g**)   Protein **0.9g**   Carbohydrate **24.4g**   Fiber **0.3g**
Cholesterol **0mg**   Iron **0.1mg**   Sodium **86mg**   Calcium **2mg**
Exchanges: ½ Starch, 1 Fruit, ½ Fat

Oatmeal-Raisin Cookies

prep: 12 minutes   cook: 9 minutes

If you bake cookies often, invest in sturdy, shiny aluminum baking sheets, large wire cooling racks, and a good metal spatula.

¾ cup granulated sugar
¼ cup packed brown sugar
⅓ cup stick margarine, softened
¼ cup apple butter
¼ cup egg substitute
½ teaspoon ground cinnamon
½ teaspoon baking soda
½ teaspoon vanilla extract
1½ cups quick-cooking oats
1 cup all-purpose flour
½ cup raisins
Cooking spray

Preheat oven to 375°.
Combine first 3 ingredients in a large bowl. Beat with a mixer at medium speed until blended. Add apple butter and next 4 ingredients, beating well. Stir in oats, flour, and raisins.
Drop dough by rounded tablespoonfuls onto baking sheets coated with cooking spray. Bake at 375° for 9 minutes or until lightly browned. Cool 1 minute on baking sheets. Remove cookies from baking sheets, and let cool completely on wire racks.
Yield: 34 cookies (serving size: 1 cookie).

Per Serving: Calories **78**   Fat **2.1g** (sat **0.4g**)   Protein **1.2g**   Carbohydrate **14.1g**   Fiber **0.6g**
Cholesterol **0mg**   Iron **0.5mg**   Sodium **43mg**   Calcium **7mg**
Exchanges: 1 Starch, ½ Fat

fish
&
shellfish

Catfish Nuggets with
Tartar Sauce *(photo, page 6)*

prep: 15 minutes   cook: 12 minutes

Say good-bye to chicken nuggets. Here's a great alternative that will help you incorporate more fish into your meal plans.

1   large egg white
2   teaspoons water
½   cup dry breadcrumbs
¼   teaspoon ground red pepper
12   ounces farm-raised catfish fillets, cut into 2-inch pieces
Butter-flavored cooking spray
2   teaspoons stick margarine, melted
¼   cup fat-free mayonnaise
2   teaspoons sweet pickle relish
2   teaspoons fresh lemon juice (about ½ lemon)
1   teaspoon Dijon mustard
Lemon wedges (optional)

Preheat oven to 450°.
Combine egg white and water in a small bowl; beat well with a whisk. Combine breadcrumbs and pepper in a shallow dish. Dip fish pieces into egg white mixture, letting excess drip off. Roll fish pieces in breadcrumb mixture to coat.
Place fish pieces on a baking sheet coated with cooking spray. Coat fish with cooking spray. Drizzle evenly with margarine.
Bake at 450° for 12 to 14 minutes or until fish flakes easily when tested with a fork.
While the fish bakes, combine mayonnaise and next 3 ingredients; stir mixture well. Serve fish with tarter sauce and, if desired, lemon wedges.
Yield: 2 servings (serving size: 6 ounces fish and 2 tablespoons sauce).

Per Serving: Calories **332** Fat **12.4g** (sat **2.6g**) Protein **34.4g** Carbohydrate **18.3g** Fiber **0.6g**
Cholesterol **98mg** Iron **2.6mg** Sodium **790mg** Calcium **102mg**
Exchanges: 1 Starch, 4 Lean Meat

Baked Catfish in Foil Packets

prep: 5 minutes   cook: 12 minutes

You can substitute flounder, orange roughy, sole, perch, or grouper for catfish in this recipe.

1½ tablespoons low-sodium soy sauce
1½ teaspoons ground ginger
1½ teaspoons sesame oil
4   (6-ounce) farm-raised catfish fillets
¼   cup sliced green onions (about 2)
½   cup chopped red bell pepper (about ½ large)
½   cup finely chopped peeled cucumber (about ½ small)

Preheat oven to 450°.
Combine soy sauce, ginger, and oil, stirring well.
Tear off 4 (12-inch) squares of aluminum foil; place a fish fillet in center of each square. Spoon green onions, bell pepper, and cucumber evenly over each fillet. Spoon soy sauce mixture evenly over vegetables. Fold foil over fillets to make packets, and seal edges tightly.
Place fish packets on a baking sheet; bake at 450° for 12 minutes or until fish flakes easily when tested with a fork.
Yield: 4 servings (serving size: 1 fillet and ⅓ cup vegetables).

Per Serving: Calories **259** Fat **14.7g** (sat **3.3g**) Protein **27.2g** Carbohydrate **3.1g** Fiber **0.8g**
Cholesterol **80mg** Iron **1.3mg** Sodium **292mg** Calcium **25mg**
Exchanges: 4 Lean Meat

Flounder in Orange Sauce

prep: 5 minutes   cook: 10 minutes

Rice and steamed asparagus are quick accompaniments to this orange-flavored fish; both can be cooked while the fish bakes.

⅓   cup low-sugar orange marmalade
2   tablespoons orange juice
¼   teaspoon ground ginger
⅓   cup sliced green onions (about 3)
4   (6-ounce) flounder fillets (or orange roughy, cod, or perch)
Cooking spray

Preheat oven to 400°.
Combine first 3 ingredients in a small saucepan. Cook over medium heat until marmalade melts, stirring often. Remove from heat, and stir in green onions.
Place fillets in a 13 x 9-inch baking dish coated with cooking spray. Spoon orange marmalade mixture evenly over fillets. Bake at 400° for 10 minutes or until fish flakes easily when tested with a fork.
Yield: 4 servings (serving size: 1 fillet).

Per Serving: Calories **210**   Fat **2.2g** (sat **0.5g**)   Protein **32.5g**   Carbohydrate **13.4g**   Fiber **0.9g**
Cholesterol **82mg**   Iron **1.1mg**   Sodium **146mg**   Calcium **46mg**
Exchanges: 1 Fruit, 4 Very Lean Meat

Flounder with Pimiento

prep: 3 minutes   cook: 12 minutes

When serving this dish, add angel hair pasta, steamed snow peas, and dinner rolls to round out the meal.

1   lemon
1   (2-ounce) jar diced pimiento, drained
4   (6-ounce) flounder fillets (or orange roughy, cod, or perch)
Butter-flavored cooking spray
1   teaspoon extraspicy salt-free herb-and-spice blend (such as
         Mrs. Dash)
Oregano sprigs (optional)

Preheat oven to 425°.
Cut lemon in half. Squeeze juice from half of lemon (about 1 table-spoon) into a small bowl; set remaining lemon half aside. Add pimiento to lemon juice, mixing well.
Place fillets in an 11 x 7-inch baking dish coated with cooking spray. Coat fish with cooking spray; sprinkle with herb-and-spice blend.
Spoon pimiento mixture evenly over fish. Bake, uncovered, at 425° for 12 minutes or until fish flakes easily when tested with a fork. While fish bakes, cut remaining lemon half into slices to serve with fish. Garnish with oregano sprigs, if desired.
Yield: 4 servings (serving size: 1 fillet).

Per Serving: Calories **164** Fat **2.2g** (sat **0.5g**) Protein **32.5g** Carbohydrate **3.6g** Fiber **1.5g**
Cholesterol **82mg** Iron **1.0mg** Sodium **141mg** Calcium **48mg**
Exchanges: 4 Very Lean Meat

Flounder with Peppers and Green Onions

prep: 7 minutes   cook: 9 minutes

A Greek salad and warm French bread add a nice finishing touch to this flounder.

2   teaspoons reduced-calorie stick margarine
⅓   cup sliced green onions (about 3)
1   teaspoon bottled minced garlic
1   red bell pepper, cut into thin strips
1½ pounds flounder fillets, cut into 4 pieces
¼   cup dry white wine
1   teaspoon grated lime rind
3   tablespoons fresh lime juice (about 2 limes)

Melt margarine in a large nonstick skillet over medium-high heat. Add green onions, garlic, and pepper strips; cook 2 minutes, stirring often. **Add** fish, and cook 2 minutes on each side. Sprinkle wine, lime rind, and lime juice over fish. Cover, reduce heat, and simmer 3 minutes or until fish flakes easily when tested with a fork. Carefully remove fish to a serving platter; top with pepper mixture.
Yield: 4 servings (serving size: 1 fillet and about ⅓ cup pepper mixture).

Per Serving: Calories **179** Fat **3.0g** (sat **0.7g**) Protein **32.6g** Carbohydrate **4.1g** Fiber **0.9g**
Cholesterol **82mg** Iron **1.0mg** Sodium **164mg** Calcium **44mg**
Exchanges: 1 Vegetable, 4 Very Lean Meat

Spicy Grouper Fillets

prep: 5 minutes   cook: 7 minutes

Serving prepackaged coleslaw and strawberry sorbet with the fish helps to get the meal on the table quickly.

2   tablespoons all-purpose flour
½   teaspoon paprika
½   teaspoon salt
¼   teaspoon ground red pepper
4   (6-ounce) grouper fillets (or red snapper or halibut)
Cooking spray
1   teaspoon olive oil
1   teaspoon minced garlic
Lemon wedges (optional)

Combine first 4 ingredients in a large heavy-duty, zip-top plastic bag. Add fillets, and turn gently to coat.
Coat a large nonstick skillet with cooking spray; add oil, and place pan over medium heat. Add garlic; sauté 30 seconds. Add fillets; cook 3 minutes on each side or until fish flakes easily when tested with a fork, removing pieces as they are done. Serve with lemon wedges, if desired.
Yield: 4 servings (serving size: 1 fillet).

Per Serving: Calories **183**   Fat **3.0g** (sat **0.6g**)   Protein **33.5g**   Carbohydrate **3.4g**   Fiber **0.2g**   Cholesterol **63mg**   Iron **1.8mg**   Sodium **381mg**   Calcium **49mg**
Exchanges: 5 Very Lean Meat

Grouper with Honey-Citrus Glaze *(photo, page 7)*

prep: 2 minutes   cook: 10 minutes

To broil instead of grill, place the fish on the rack of a broiler pan coated with cooking spray. Broil 5 minutes on each side, basting occasionally with the orange juice mixture. This dish is especially delicious when served with steamed asparagus and French bread slices.

3 tablespoons orange juice concentrate, thawed and undiluted
2 tablespoons honey
1 teaspoon dried basil
¼ teaspoon garlic powder
6 dashes of hot sauce
4 (6-ounce) grouper fillets (or red snapper or halibut)
Cooking spray
Orange rind strips (optional)

Prepare grill.
Combine first 5 ingredients, stirring well.
Arrange fillets in a wire grilling basket coated with cooking spray. Place grilling basket on grill rack; cover and grill 5 minutes on each side or until fish flakes easily when tested with a fork, basting occasionally with orange juice mixture. Transfer fillets to a serving platter. Garnish with orange rind, if desired.
Yield: 4 servings (serving size: 1 fillet).

Per Serving: Calories **212** Fat **1.8g** (sat **0.4g**) Protein **33.4g** Carbohydrate **14.2g** Fiber **0.3g**
Cholesterol **63mg** Iron **1.8mg** Sodium **99mg** Calcium **59mg**
Exchanges: 1 Fruit, 4 Very Lean Meat

Asian-Style Grouper

prep: 3 minutes   cook: 11 minutes

It's fine to substitute ⅓ cup of white wine for the sherry; the flavor just won't be quite as sweet. Serve with rice and steamed baby carrots.

Garlic-flavored cooking spray
4   (6-ounce) grouper fillets (or red snapper or halibut)
⅓   cup low-sodium soy sauce
⅓   cup dry sherry
2   teaspoons sugar
¼   cup sliced green onions (about 2)

Heat a large nonstick skillet coated with cooking spray over medium-high heat. Add fillets, and cook 4 minutes on each side or until fish flakes easily when tested with a fork; remove fillets from pan, and keep warm.

Combine soy sauce, sherry, and sugar; add mixture to hot pan. Cook over high heat 3 minutes or until mixture thickens, stirring constantly to loosen particles that cling to bottom of pan.

Return fillets to pan, turning to coat with glaze. Transfer fillets to each of 4 serving plates; sprinkle green onions evenly over fish, and serve immediately.

Yield: 4 servings (serving size: 1 fillet).

Per Serving: Calories 179   Fat **1.8g** (sat **0.4g**)   Protein **34.2g**   Carbohydrate **4.6g**   Fiber **0.3g**
Cholesterol **63mg**   Iron **2.1mg**   Sodium **804mg**   Calcium **56mg**
Exchanges: 5 Very Lean Meat

Wine-Baked Orange Roughy

prep: 4 minutes   cook: 10 minutes

Serve the orange roughy with a spinach salad and French baguette slices.

4   (6-ounce) orange roughy fillets (or flounder, perch, or sole)
Cooking spray
¼   teaspoon salt
¼   teaspoon freshly ground black pepper
⅛   teaspoon garlic powder
¼   cup sliced green onions (about 2)
1   (2-ounce) jar diced pimiento, drained
¼   cup lemon juice
¼   cup dry white wine

Preheat oven to 400°.
Place fillets in an 11 x 7-inch baking dish coated with cooking spray; sprinkle fillets evenly with salt, pepper, garlic powder, green onions, and pimiento. Pour lemon juice and wine over fillets.
Cover and bake at 400° for 10 minutes or until fish flakes easily when tested with a fork. Serve with a slotted spatula.
Yield: 4 servings (serving size: 1 fillet).

Per Serving: Calories **128**   Fat **1.3g** (sat **0.0g**)   Protein **25.4g**   Carbohydrate **2.9g**   Fiber **0.5g**
Cholesterol **34mg**   Iron **0.7mg**   Sodium **258mg**   Calcium **59mg**
Exchanges: 4 Very Lean Meat

Dijon Orange Roughy

prep: 2 minutes   cook: 12 minutes

Dijon mustard has a strong, distinctive flavor. For a flavor variation, use honey mustard, sweet-hot mustard, or spicy mustard. Serve with couscous and steamed broccoli.

1	(12-ounce) orange roughy fillet (or flounder, perch, or sole)

Butter-flavored cooking spray

1½	tablespoons Dijon mustard
2	teaspoons lemon juice
1½	teaspoons low-sodium Worcestershire sauce
3	tablespoons Italian-seasoned breadcrumbs

Preheat oven to 450°.

Arrange fillet in an 11 x 7-inch baking dish coated with cooking spray. Combine mustard, lemon juice, and Worcestershire sauce, stirring well; spread mixture evenly over fillet. Sprinkle breadcrumbs evenly over fillet.

Bake at 450° for 12 minutes or until fish flakes easily when tested with a fork. Cut fillet in half, and serve immediately.

Yield: 2 servings (serving size: ½ fillet).

Per Serving: Calories **175** Fat **2.5g** (sat **0.2g**) Protein **27.4g** Carbohydrate **9.9g** Fiber **0.6g**
Cholesterol **34mg** Iron **1.0mg** Sodium **694mg** Calcium **79mg**
Exchanges: ½ Starch, 4 Very Lean Meat

Seaside Stir-Fry

prep: 7 minutes   cook: 6 minutes

Put a regular-sized bag of quick-cooking rice on to cook before you start preparing this recipe. It will be done in 10 minutes and yield 2 cups of cooked rice. Refrigerate or freeze the extra cup of rice; it reheats well in the microwave. Serve with sesame breadsticks.

Cooking spray
1   teaspoon sesame oil
3   tablespoons low-sodium soy sauce
1   teaspoon cornstarch
½   teaspoon ground ginger
¼   teaspoon garlic powder
3   green onions, cut into 2-inch pieces
1   carrot, scraped and sliced
1   red bell pepper, cut into thin strips
12   ounces orange roughy fillets (or flounder, perch, or sole), cut into
        bite-sized pieces
1   cup hot cooked rice

Coat a wok or medium-sized nonstick skillet with cooking spray; add oil. Place over medium-high heat. While wok heats, combine soy sauce, cornstarch, ginger, and garlic powder, stirring well; set aside. **Add** vegetables to hot wok, and stir-fry 3 minutes or until crisp-tender. Add fish, and stir-fry 1 minute. Stir soy sauce mixture; add to wok. Reduce heat to medium-low, and cook 2 minutes, tossing often or until soy sauce mixture is slightly thickened and fish flakes easily when tested with a fork. Serve immediately over hot cooked rice.
Yield: 2 servings.

Per Serving: Calories **277** Fat **3.8g** (sat **0.4g**) Protein **30.0g** Carbohydrate **30.2g** Fiber **3.8g**
Cholesterol **34mg** Iron **1.9mg** Sodium **927mg** Calcium **78mg**
Exchanges: 2 Starch, 3 Very Lean Meat

Teriyaki-Glazed Salmon with Peach Salsa *(photo, back cover)*

prep: 9 minutes   cook: 6 minutes

Serve with steamed asparagus drizzled with lemon juice.

3   tablespoons low-sodium teriyaki sauce
2   tablespoons lime juice
1½ tablespoons honey
4   (6-ounce) salmon fillets, skinned
1½ cups frozen peach slices, thawed and chopped, or 1½ cups drained
        and chopped canned peaches
¼   cup minced fresh cilantro or mint
2   teaspoons honey
1   teaspoon lime juice
Cooking spray

Prepare grill.
Combine first 3 ingredients in a shallow dish; stir well. Add fillets,
and let stand 5 minutes.
While fillets marinate, combine peach slices and next 3 ingredients
in a small bowl; stir well. Set aside.
Remove fillets from marinade, discarding marinade. Place fillets on a
grill rack or in a grill basket coated with cooking spray; grill 3 to 5
minutes on each side or until fish flakes easily when tested with a fork.
Remove fish from grill, and top with peach mixture.
Yield: 4 servings (serving size: 1 fillet and about ⅓ cup salsa).

Per Serving: Calories 270   Fat **6.0g** (sat **1.0g**)   Protein **34.5g**   Carbohydrate **19.0g**   Fiber **1.4g**
Cholesterol **88mg**   Iron **1.6mg**   Sodium **311mg**   Calcium **31mg**
Exchanges: 1 Fruit, 5 Very Lean Meat

Salmon with Pineapple Salsa

prep: 5 minutes   cook: 8 minutes

Try serving the salmon with rice and roasted zucchini and yellow squash strips.

4 (6-ounce) salmon fillets (½ inch thick), skinned
Cooking spray
1 tablespoon low-sodium soy sauce
1 (20-ounce) can pineapple tidbits in juice, drained
½ cup finely chopped green bell pepper (about ½ large)
¼ cup finely chopped red onion (about ½ small)
1 jalapeño pepper, seeded and minced
1 tablespoon fresh lime juice (about 1 lime)

Preheat broiler.

Arrange fillets on rack of a broiler pan coated with cooking spray; brush fillets with soy sauce. Broil 4 minutes on each side or until fish flakes easily when tested with a fork.

While salmon broils, combine pineapple and remaining 4 ingredients in a small bowl.

Transfer salmon fillets to a serving platter; top with salsa.

Yield: 4 servings (serving size: 1 fillet and about ¾ cup salsa).

Per Serving: Calories **244**   Fat **6.1g** (sat **1.0g**)   Protein **34.9g**   Carbohydrate **11.5g**   Fiber **1.4g**
Cholesterol **88mg**   Iron **1.9mg**   Sodium **250mg**   Calcium **42mg**
Exchanges: 1 Fruit, 4 Lean Meat

Salmon with Cucumber-Dill Sauce

prep: 5 minutes   cook: 11 minutes

Salmon steaks come with the skin on. To help the steaks hold an attractive shape, cook and serve the salmon without removing the skin. Serve the salmon with New Potatoes in Seasoned Butter (recipe on page 233) and steamed asparagus.

1   cup dry white wine
½   cup water
1   tablespoon lemon juice
4   (6-ounce) salmon steaks (½ inch thick), skinned
¾   cup plain fat-free yogurt
½   cup unpeeled finely chopped cucumber (about ½ small)
1   teaspoon dried dill or 1 tablespoon chopped fresh dill
¼   teaspoon salt

Combine first 3 ingredients in a large nonstick skillet; stir well. Bring mixture to a boil over medium heat. Reduce heat to low, and add salmon steaks to pan. Simmer 8 minutes or until fish flakes easily when tested with a fork.
While salmon cooks, combine yogurt, cucumber, dill, and salt; stir well.
Gently transfer salmon to a serving platter, using two spatulas; spoon cucumber sauce over each steak.
Yield: 4 servings (serving size: 1 steak and ⅓ cup sauce).

Per Serving: Calories **271**   Fat **11.0g** (sat **1.7g**)   Protein **36.4g**   Carbohydrate **5.2g**   Fiber **0.2g**
Cholesterol **97mg**   Iron **1.8mg**   Sodium **253mg**   Calcium **88mg**
Exchanges: 1 Vegetable, 5 Lean Meat

Spicy Lemon Red Snapper

prep: 6 minutes   cook: 6 minutes

Serve this spicy, lemony snapper with green beans and Corn Muffins (recipe on page 65).

4   (6-ounce) red snapper fillets
¼   cup fresh lemon juice (about 2 lemons)
1   teaspoon black and red pepper blend (such as McCormick's)
1   teaspoon dry mustard
1   teaspoon onion powder
1   teaspoon dried thyme
Cooking spray
Lemon wedges (optional)

Prepare grill.
Place fillets in a large shallow dish; pour lemon juice over fillets. Let stand 5 minutes.
While fish marinates, combine pepper blend and next 3 ingredients. Remove fillets from lemon juice, discarding juice. Rub pepper mixture over both sides of fillets.
Place fillets on a grill rack or in a grill basket coated with cooking spray; cover and grill 3 minutes on each side or until fish flakes easily when tested with a fork. Serve with lemon wedges, if desired.
Yield: 4 servings (serving size: 1 fillet).

Per Serving: Calories **182** Fat **2.6g** (sat **0.5g**) Protein **35.3g** Carbohydrate **2.4g** Fiber **0.4g**
Cholesterol **63mg** Iron **0.9mg** Sodium **110mg** Calcium **67mg**
Exchanges: 5 Very Lean Meat

Garlic-Baked Snapper

prep: 11 minutes   cook: 15 minutes

To test fish for doneness, flake it with a fork at its thickest point. Properly cooked fish flakes easily and appears opaque with milky white juices. To make fresh breadcrumbs, place 1½ slices of white bread in a food processor; pulse 10 times or until coarse crumbs measure 1 cup.

4   (6-ounce) red snapper fillets
Cooking spray
1½ tablespoons dry sherry
1   cup dry breadcrumbs
3   tablespoons chopped fresh parsley
¾   teaspoon paprika
½   teaspoon ground red pepper
1   or 2 garlic cloves, minced
Lemon wedges (optional)

Preheat oven to 400°.

Place fillets in an 11 x 7-inch baking dish coated with cooking spray; drizzle with sherry.

Combine breadcrumbs and next 4 ingredients; sprinkle evenly over fillets. Bake at 400° for 15 to 20 minutes or until fish flakes easily when tested with a fork. Serve with lemon wedges, if desired.

Yield: 4 servings (serving size: 1 fillet).

Per Serving: Calories **199** Fat **2.8g** (sat **0.6g**) Protein **35.9g** Carbohydrate **5.2g** Fiber **0.4g**
Cholesterol **63mg** Iron **0.9mg** Sodium **160mg** Calcium **69mg**
Exchanges: ½ Starch, 5 Very Lean Meat

Trout with Almonds

prep: 2 minutes   cook: 8 minutes

This recipe is higher in fat than most fish entrées, but the fats are mostly monounsaturated and polyunsaturated—the heart-healthy types of fat. Traditional trout almondine contains about 54 grams of fat per serving. Our version here has only 17.3 grams.

¼   cup all-purpose flour
¼   teaspoon salt
¼   teaspoon pepper
4   (6-ounce) trout fillets
3   tablespoons yogurt-based spread (such as Brummel & Brown),
        divided
2   tablespoons fresh lemon juice (about 1 lemon)
2   tablespoons chopped fresh parsley
¼   cup slivered almonds, toasted

Combine first 3 ingredients in a large heavy-duty zip-top plastic bag. Add fillets; seal bag, and turn gently to coat.

Heat 1 tablespoon spread in a large nonstick skillet over medium-high heat. Add fillets to pan; cook, turning once, 5 to 6 minutes, or until fish flakes easily when tested with a fork. Set fish aside, and keep warm.

Add remaining 2 tablespoons spread, lemon juice, and parsley to pan. Bring to a simmer. Spoon sauce over fish; sprinkle with almonds.

Yield: 4 servings (serving size: 1 fillet, 1 tablespoon sauce, and 1 tablespoon almonds).

Per Serving: Calories **351** Fat **17.3g** (sat **3.7g**) Protein **38.2g** Carbohydrate **8.5g** Fiber **1.1g**
Cholesterol **100mg** Iron **1.3mg** Sodium **276mg** Calcium **140mg**
Exchanges: ½ Starch, 5 Lean Meat, 1 Fat

Chipotle-Chutney Tuna Steaks

prep: 6 minutes   cook: 9 minutes

Grill these tuna steaks instead of broiling, if you prefer. Place fish on a grill rack coated with cooking spray; cover and grill 4 minutes on each side.

¼ cup mango chutney
1   to 2 teaspoons minced canned chipotle chiles in adobo sauce
        (or 2 teaspoons fresh lime juice plus ¼ teaspoon ground red pepper)
4   (6-ounce) tuna steaks
Cooking spray
2   tablespoons chopped fresh cilantro

Preheat broiler.

Combine chutney and chiles in a small bowl. Place steaks on rack of a broiler pan coated with cooking spray; spread half of chutney mixture evenly over steaks.

Broil steaks 5 minutes. Turn steaks over; brush with remaining chutney mixture. Broil an additional 4 to 5 minutes or until fish flakes easily when tested with a fork.

Place steaks on each of 4 serving plates; sprinkle cilantro evenly over fish.

Yield: 4 servings (serving size: 1 steak).

Per Serving: Calories **291**   Fat **8.4g** (sat **2.1g**)   Protein **39.7g**   Carbohydrate **11.3g**   Fiber **0.0g**
Cholesterol **66mg**   Iron **1.9mg**   Sodium **319mg**   Calcium **15mg**
Exchanges: 1 Starch, 5 Very Lean Meat

Grilled Tuna Kebabs

prep: 5 minutes   cook: 8 minutes

Serve with Mediterranean Couscous (recipe on page 243) and a bean salad.

12   ounces tuna steaks, trimmed and cut into 1-inch pieces
1   green bell pepper, cut into 1-inch pieces (about 1 cup)
1   cup pineapple chunks
¼   cup lemon juice
¼   cup dry white wine
2   teaspoons minced garlic
1   teaspoon dried oregano
1   teaspoon olive oil
½   teaspoon salt
Cooking spray

Prepare grill.
Thread first 3 ingredients alternately onto 4 (12-inch) metal skewers. Combine lemon juice and next 5 ingredients, stirring well; brush over kebabs.
Place kebabs on grill rack coated with cooking spray; cover and grill 8 to 12 minutes or until fish flakes easily when tested with a fork, turning and basting with lemon juice mixture.
Yield: 2 servings (serving size: 2 kebabs).

Per Serving: Calories **335**   Fat **11.1g** (sat **2.5g**)   Protein **40.9g**   Carbohydrate **17.9g**   Fiber **2.5g**   Cholesterol **65mg**   Iron **2.8mg**   Sodium **658mg**   Calcium **46mg**
Exchanges: 1 Fruit, 5 Lean Meat

Creamy Skillet Tuna Casserole

prep: 5 minutes   cook: 15 minutes

We suggest serving this comforting casserole with a mixed green salad and finishing off the meal with a slice of apple pie.

6   ounces uncooked egg noodles
1   (10¾-ounce) can condensed reduced-fat, reduced-sodium cream
        of mushroom soup, undiluted
½   cup fat-free, less-sodium chicken broth
½   cup evaporated fat-free milk
¼   teaspoon pepper
¾   cup frozen chopped onion
1   cup frozen green peas
2   (6-ounce) cans low-sodium tuna in water, drained
1   (2-ounce) jar diced pimiento, drained
¼   cup grated Parmesan cheese

Cook noodles according to package directions, omitting salt and fat.
Combine soup and next 3 ingredients in a large skillet, stirring until smooth. Stir in onion; bring to a boil over medium heat, stirring often. Reduce heat, and simmer, uncovered, 5 minutes or until onion is tender.
Drain noodles. Add noodles, peas, tuna, and pimiento to pan, and stir. Simmer 5 minutes or until thoroughly heated, stirring occasionally. Spoon onto each of 4 serving plates, and sprinkle evenly with cheese.
Yield: 5 servings (serving size: about 1¾ cups).

Per Serving: Calories **292**   Fat **4.4g** (sat **2.1g**)   Protein **22.7g**   Carbohydrate **38.8g**   Fiber **3.9g**
Cholesterol **54mg**   Iron **2.9mg**   Sodium **459mg**   Calcium **194mg**
Exchanges: 2½ Starch, 2 Lean Meat

Lemon-Dill Scallops
and Snow Peas

prep: 6 minutes   cook: 5 minutes

When fresh snow peas aren't available, use frozen sugar snap peas instead. Serve with a fresh fruit salad of strawberries, peaches, and pineapple.

Cooking spray
2   teaspoons reduced-calorie stick margarine
12   ounces bay scallops
6   ounces snow peas, trimmed at stem end
⅛   teaspoon salt
¼   teaspoon dried dill or ¾ teaspoon chopped fresh dill
2   teaspoons fresh lemon juice

Lightly coat a nonstick skillet with cooking spray; add margarine, and place over high heat until margarine melts. Add scallops; cook 2 minutes, stirring often. Add snow peas and remaining ingredients; cook 2 minutes, stirring often. Serve immediately.
Yield: 2 servings.

Per Serving: Calories **203**   Fat **3.3g** (sat **0.5g**)   Protein **31.0g**   Carbohydrate **11.0g**   Fiber **2.3g**
Cholesterol **56mg**   Iron **2.3mg**   Sodium **470mg**   Calcium **81mg**
Exchanges: 2 Vegetable, 4 Very Lean Meat

Spicy Baked Shrimp

prep: 4 minutes   cook: 8 minutes

Rinse a measuring spoon or cup with cold water or spray with cooking spray before measuring honey; the honey will slide out easily. Corn on the cob and coleslaw pair nicely with this quick-and-easy shrimp.

Olive oil-flavored cooking spray
2   tablespoons lemon juice
1   tablespoon honey
2   teaspoons dried parsley flakes
2   teaspoons salt-free Creole seasoning
1   teaspoon olive oil
2   teaspoons low-sodium soy sauce
¾   pound large peeled and deveined shrimp (about 1 pound unpeeled)

Preheat oven to 450°.
Coat an 11 x 7-inch baking dish with cooking spray. Add lemon juice and next 5 ingredients to dish, stirring well. Add shrimp; toss well to coat. Bake at 450° for 8 minutes or until shrimp are done, stirring occasionally.
Yield: 2 servings.

Per Serving: Calories **239**   Fat **5.2g** (sat **0.4g**)   Protein **34.9g**   Carbohydrate **12.1g**   Fiber **0.1g**
Cholesterol **259mg**   Iron **4.3mg**   Sodium **430mg**   Calcium **92mg**
Exchanges: 1 Starch, 4 Very Lean Meat

Skillet Barbecued Shrimp

prep: 1 minute   cook: 10 minutes

Serve with corn on the cob and a spinach-orange salad. For fresh citrus flavor, toss orange sections with the spinach before drizzling with fat-free poppy seed dressing.

1   family-sized bag quick-cooking boil-in-bag rice or 3 cups
        hot cooked rice
1½ pounds large peeled and deveined shrimp (about 2 pounds
        unpeeled)
1   tablespoon no-salt-added Creole seasoning (such as
        Tony Chachere's)
Cooking spray
½   cup chili sauce (such as Heinz)
½   teaspoon hot sauce

Cook rice according to package directions, omitting salt and fat.
While rice cooks, toss shrimp with Creole seasoning. Coat a large
nonstick skillet with cooking spray; place over medium-high heat.
Add shrimp; cook 3 to 5 minutes or until shrimp are done, stirring
often. Add chili sauce and hot sauce; reduce heat, and cook 2 minutes.
Serve over rice.
Yield: 4 servings (serving size: 6 ounces shrimp and ¾ cup rice).

Per Serving: Calories **342**   Fat **3.2g** (sat **0.6g**)   Protein **37.1g**   Carbohydrate **37.9g**   Fiber **0.8g**
Cholesterol **259mg**   Iron **4.9mg**   Sodium **1,219mg**   Calcium **98mg**
Exchanges: 2½ Starch, 4 Very Lean Meat

Thai Shrimp with Basil

prep: 9 minutes   cook: 6 minutes

Brown rice and soft garlic breadsticks are delicious side items for this Thai-inspired dish.

1½ pounds large peeled and deveined shrimp (about 2 pounds
       unpeeled)
1   tablespoon minced peeled fresh ginger
Garlic-flavored cooking spray
1   cup (1½-inch-long) carrot sticks (half of an 8-ounce package
       carrot sticks)
¼   teaspoon dried crushed red pepper
6   ounces snow peas, trimmed at stem end
⅓   cup low-sodium teriyaki sauce
¼   cup thinly sliced fresh basil

Toss shrimp with ginger; set aside.
Heat a large nonstick skillet coated with cooking spray over medium-high heat. Add carrot sticks, and cook 2 minutes, stirring often. Add shrimp mixture; stir-fry 2 minutes. Add red pepper, snow peas, and teriyaki sauce; stir-fry 2 minutes or until shrimp are done. Stir in basil.
Yield: 4 servings (serving size: about 1½ cups).

Per Serving: Calories **227** Fat **3.1g** (sat **0.6g**) Protein **36.2g** Carbohydrate **11.0g** Fiber **2.2g**
Cholesterol **259mg** Iron **5.4mg** Sodium **611mg** Calcium **122mg**
Exchanges: 2 Vegetable, 5 Very Lean Meat

Cold Sesame Shrimp and Pasta

prep: 11 minutes   cook: 11 minutes

Cooking the pasta and shrimp together in the same water saves time and cleanup, plus it adds flavor to the pasta. Prepare the cucumber, green onions, and peanuts while the pasta and shrimp cook. It's a great way to cut down on time spent in the kitchen. Serve with sliced fresh tomatoes and breadsticks.

8   ounces uncooked vermicelli
1½   pounds large peeled and deveined shrimp (about 2 pounds
         unpeeled)
1½   teaspoons sesame oil
¼   cup seasoned rice vinegar
1   small cucumber, quartered lengthwise and sliced
½   cup diagonally sliced green onions (1-inch pieces) (about 4 large)
¼   teaspoon crushed red pepper
1   tablespoon chopped dry-roasted peanuts

Bring 2 quarts water to a boil in a large saucepan. Break pasta in half, add to boiling water, and cook 3 minutes. (Do not add salt or fat.)
Add shrimp to pasta, and cook 3 minutes or until shrimp are done. Drain pasta mixture; rinse under cold water until cool. Drain again. Transfer pasta and shrimp to a large bowl.
Add oil, vinegar, cucumber, green onions, and crushed pepper to pasta mixture; toss gently. Arrange pasta mixture on each of 4 serving plates; sprinkle peanuts evenly over each serving.
Yield: 4 servings (serving size: about 2¼ cups).

Per Serving: Calories **446** Fat **6.9g** (sat **1.1g**) Protein **43.7g** Carbohydrate **49.9g** Fiber **4.0g**
Cholesterol **259mg** Iron **6.8mg** Sodium **266mg** Calcium **126mg**
Exchanges: 3 Starch, 1 Vegetable, 5 Very Lean Meat

meatless main dishes

Mediterranean Pizza

prep: 4 minutes   cook: 12 minutes

Serve with a romaine lettuce salad tossed with fat-free raspberry vinaigrette.

1   (7-ounce) container refrigerated hummus
1   (10-ounce) Italian cheese-flavored thin pizza crust
        (such as Boboli)
1   (7-ounce) bottle roasted red bell peppers, drained and chopped
1   (14-ounce) can quartered artichoke hearts, drained and coarsely
        chopped
4   kalamata olives, pitted and chopped
½   cup (2 ounces) crumbled feta cheese with basil and sun-dried
        tomatoes

Preheat oven to 450°.

Spread hummus over crust; arrange peppers and remaining ingredients over hummus.

Bake at 450° for 12 to 14 minutes or until cheese softens and pizza is thoroughly heated.

Yield: 6 servings (serving size: 1 slice).

Per Serving: Calories **265** Fat **9.7g** (sat **2.8g**) Protein **11.9g** Carbohydrate **34.0g** Fiber **2.7g**
Cholesterol **2mg** Iron **1.9mg** Sodium **561mg** Calcium **220mg**
Exchanges: 2 Starch, 1 Vegetable, ½ Medium-Fat Meat, 1 Fat

Vegetable-Cheese Pizza

prep: 4 minutes   cook: 10 minutes

*You can use any flavor of flatbread or focaccia, or even individual
flatbread crusts for this recipe.*

Cooking spray
2   medium green bell peppers, cut into thin strips
1   small onion (about 3 ounces), thinly sliced
1   (8-ounce) package presliced mushrooms
1   cup pizza sauce
1   (12.5-ounce) sun-dried tomato-flavored flatbread
5   (1-ounce) slices provolone cheese

Preheat oven to 425°.
Heat a large nonstick skillet coated with cooking spray over
medium-high heat. Add peppers, onion, and mushrooms; cook 8
minutes or until tender, stirring often.
While vegetables cook, spread pizza sauce over flatbread. Place
directly on middle oven rack, and bake at 425° for 5 minutes.
Top pizza with vegetable mixture. Arrange cheese over vegetables,
and bake 2 minutes or until cheese melts.
Yield: 6 servings (serving size: 1 slice).

Per Serving: Calories **262** Fat **7.4g** (sat **4.1g**) Protein **13.3g** Carbohydrate **35.0g** Fiber **2.1g**
Cholesterol **16mg** Iron **1.1mg** Sodium **617mg** Calcium **186mg**
Exchanges: 2 Starch, 1 Vegetable, 1 High-Fat Meat

Tomato-Feta Omelet

prep: 4 minutes   cook: 6 minutes

*Add Fruit and Honey Spinach Salad (recipe on page 201) and warm
pita bread to the menu, and breakfast becomes dinner in a flash.*

1   (8-ounce) carton egg substitute
⅛   teaspoon salt
⅛   teaspoon pepper
Olive oil-flavored cooking spray
2   tablespoons finely chopped red onion (about ½ small)
2   medium plum tomatoes, chopped
¼   cup (1-ounce) crumbled garlic- and herb-flavored feta cheese

Combine first 3 ingredients in a medium bowl, stirring well with
a whisk.
Heat a medium nonstick skillet coated with cooking spray over
medium-high heat. Add onion, and sauté until tender; remove from
pan, and set aside. Reduce heat to medium; add egg substitute mixture
to pan. Carefully lift edges of omelet using a spatula; allow uncooked
portion to flow underneath cooked portion. Cook until omelet is softly
set; remove from heat.
Spoon onion, tomato, and cheese onto center of omelet. Fold one-third
of omelet over filling, and slide omelet onto a plate; fold remaining
one-third omelet over top. Cut omelet in half.
Yield: 2 servings.

Per Serving: Calories **117** Fat **3.4g** (sat **2.2g**) Protein **14.7g** Carbohydrate **6.5g** Fiber **1.0g**
Cholesterol **13mg** Iron **2.6mg** Sodium **490mg** Calcium **116mg**
Exchanges: 1 Vegetable, 2 Lean Meat

Cheese and Vegetable Omelet

prep: 3 minutes   cook: 9 minutes

Serve this vegetarian-style omelet with toasted English muffins and sliced tomatoes.

Butter-flavored cooking spray
1¾ cups finely chopped zucchini (about 1 small)
¼   teaspoon dried dill
1   (8-ounce) carton egg substitute
⅓   cup thinly sliced green onions (about 3)
¼   teaspoon freshly ground black pepper
⅛   teaspoon salt
½   cup (2 ounces) preshredded reduced-fat Cheddar cheese

Heat a 10-inch nonstick skillet coated with cooking spray over medium-high heat. Add zucchini, and cook 4 minutes or until crisp-tender, stirring occasionally. Stir in dill; remove mixture from pan, and set aside. Wipe pan with paper towels.
Coat same pan with cooking spray; place over medium-high heat until hot. Combine egg substitute and next 3 ingredients, stirring well. Add egg substitute mixture to pan, and cook 2 minutes. Carefully lift edges of omelet using a spatula; allow uncooked portion to flow underneath cooked portion. Cook 2 minutes or until center is almost set.
Spoon cheese and zucchini mixture down center of omelet. Fold omelet in half. Reduce heat to low; cook 1 minute or until cheese melts and omelet is set. Cut omelet in half.
Yield: 2 servings.

Per Serving: Calories **168** Fat **5.9g** (sat **3.2g**) Protein **21.9g** Carbohydrate **6.9g** Fiber **1.0g**
Cholesterol **18mg** Iron **3.0mg** Sodium **542mg** Calcium **293mg**
Exchanges: 1 Vegetable, 3 Lean Meat

Egg Olé Burritos

prep: 7 minutes   cook: 4 minutes

Pair this spicy burrito with steamed green beans and cantaloupe slices.

1   (8-ounce) carton egg substitute
¼   teaspoon salt
¼   teaspoon pepper
Cooking spray
¼   cup (1 ounce) preshredded reduced-fat Cheddar cheese
4   (8-inch) flour tortillas
½   cup thick and chunky salsa
¼   cup fat-free sour cream
2   tablespoons chopped fresh cilantro or parsley

Combine first 3 ingredients in a small bowl. Heat a large nonstick skillet coated with cooking spray over medium heat. Add egg mixture; cook until mixture is softly set, stirring often. Remove from heat, and top with cheese.

Spoon egg substitute mixture evenly over tortillas; top with salsa, sour cream, and cilantro. Roll up tortillas; place, seam sides down, on a serving platter.

Yield: 4 servings (serving size: 1 burrito).

Per Serving: Calories 200   Fat **3.6g** (sat **0.8g**)   Protein **11.2g**   Carbohydrate **20.1g**   Fiber **1.6g**
Cholesterol **5mg**   Iron **1.5mg**   Sodium **685mg**   Calcium **86mg**
Exchanges: 1½ Starch, 1 Lean Meat

Open-Faced Eggwich

prep: 6 minutes   cook: 9 minutes

Egg yolks are less likely to break if you crack the eggs over a saucer.
To crack gently, tap each egg firmly with the sharp edge of a table knife.

Cheddar Cheese Sauce
4   large eggs
2   English muffins, split
4   slices tomato
3   tablespoons honey mustard

Preheat broiler.
Add water to a medium skillet to depth of 2 inches; bring to a boil.
(While water comes to a boil, prepare Cheddar Cheese Sauce.) Reduce
heat to low. Break eggs, one at a time, into a saucer; slip eggs, one at
a time, into simmering water, holding saucer as close as possible to
surface of water. Simmer 6 to 7 minutes or until internal temperature
of egg reaches 160° (yolk will be solid).
While eggs simmer, place muffin halves and tomato slices on a baking
sheet; broil 4 minutes or until muffins are toasted and tomato slices
are warm. Spread muffins with mustard; top each with a tomato slice.
Remove eggs from water with a slotted spoon, and place over tomato
slices; top with Cheddar Cheese Sauce.
Yield: 4 servings (serving size: 1 eggwich and 2 tablespoons sauce).

Cheddar Cheese Sauce
½   cup low-fat milk
2   teaspoons all-purpose flour
¼   cup (1 ounce) preshredded reduced-fat sharp Cheddar cheese
⅛   teaspoon salt

Combine milk and flour in a small saucepan. Cook over medium heat,
stirring constantly, until thickened and bubbly. Add cheese and salt,
stirring until cheese melts.
Yield: ½ cup.

Per Serving: Calories **297**   Fat **9.3g** (sat **2.6g**)   Protein **14.6g**   Carbohydrate **39.6g**   Fiber **0.7g**
Cholesterol **227mg**   Iron **2.7mg**   Sodium **592mg**   Calcium **219mg**
Exchanges: 2½ Starch, 1 High-Fat Meat

Cheese and Chile Tortilla Stack

prep: 9 minutes   cook: 6 minutes

A fruit plate of sliced pears and red grapes is a simple side for this dish. Sprinkle the pear slices with lime juice, and top with grapes. Dust with a little powdered sugar right before serving.

3   (8-inch) fat-free flour tortillas
Cooking spray
1½ cups (6 ounces) preshredded part-skim mozzarella cheese
1   tablespoon plus 1 teaspoon chopped canned jalapeño pepper, drained
¾   cup chopped green onions (about 5), divided
2   cups shredded iceberg lettuce
¼   cup fat-free sour cream
¼   cup thick and chunky salsa
2   tablespoons chopped fresh cilantro or parsley

Preheat oven to 400°.
Place 1 tortilla on a baking sheet coated with cooking spray; sprinkle with ¾ cup cheese, 2 teaspoons jalapeño pepper, and ¼ cup onions. Top with another tortilla, pressing down gently. Sprinkle with remaining cheese, remaining pepper, and ¼ cup onions. Top with remaining tortilla, pressing down gently. Coat tortilla stack with cooking spray.
Bake at 400° for 6 to 8 minutes or until cheese melts; remove from oven, and transfer to a serving platter. Cut stack in half, and top evenly with lettuce, sour cream, and salsa. Sprinkle evenly with remaining ¼ cup green onions and cilantro.
Yield: 2 servings.

Per Serving: Calories **447**   Fat **13.8g** (sat **8.7g**)   Protein **30.6g**   Carbohydrate **48.3g**   Fiber **6.6g**
Cholesterol **50mg**   Iron **1.8mg**   Sodium **905mg**   Calcium **596mg**
Exchanges: 3 Starch, 1 Vegetable, 3 Medium-Fat Meat

Brown Rice-Vegetable Burritos

prep: 5 minutes   cook: 11 minutes

Serve with pineapple wedges and steamed corn on the cob. For a flavor kick, sprinkle salt-free lemon pepper seasoning on the corn.

1   (3 ½-ounce) bag boil-in-bag brown rice
Cooking spray
1   cup chopped yellow squash (about 1 small)
¼   cup chopped red onion (about ½ small)
1   cup drained canned chickpeas (garbanzo beans)
½   cup chopped tomato (1 small)
6   (8-inch) fat-free flour tortillas
1   (12-ounce) jar fat-free black bean dip

Cook rice according to package directions; set aside to drain.
While rice cooks, heat a large nonstick skillet coated with cooking spray over medium-high heat. Add squash and onion; cook 5 minutes or until crisp-tender, stirring often. Combine squash mixture, chickpeas, tomato, and cooked rice, stirring gently.
Wrap tortillas in heavy-duty plastic wrap, and microwave at HIGH 1 minute or until warm. Spread 2 tablespoons bean dip over each tortilla. Spoon ¾ cup rice mixture down center of each tortilla; fold in 1 side, and roll up.
Yield: 6 servings (serving size: 1 burrito).

Per Serving: Calories **308**   Fat **1.6g** (sat **0.0g**)   Protein **13.2g**   Carbohydrate **59.7g**   Fiber **8.0g**
Cholesterol **0mg**   Iron **1.5mg**   Sodium **510mg**   Calcium **66mg**
Exchanges: 3 Starch, 1 Vegetable, 1 Very Lean Meat

Rice and Bean Soft Tacos

prep: 7 minutes   cook: 10 minutes

Leftover rice works well in this recipe. Or use quick-cooking rice that cooks in just 10 minutes. Serve with kiwifruit slices and strawberries.

4   (10-inch) flour tortillas
Cooking spray
½   cup thinly sliced green bell pepper (about ½ small)
½   cup thinly sliced onion (about ½ medium)
1   cup hot cooked long-grain rice
1   (15-ounce) can no-salt-added black beans, rinsed and drained
⅓   cup salsa
½   teaspoon chili powder
⅛   teaspoon salt
½   cup fat-free sour cream
¼   cup (1 ounce) shredded Monterey Jack cheese with jalapeño
      peppers

Preheat oven to 350°.
Wrap tortillas in aluminum foil. Bake at 350° for 10 minutes or until tortillas are warm.
While tortillas bake, heat a nonstick skillet coated with cooking spray over medium-high heat. Add bell pepper and onion; cook 4 minutes or until tender, stirring often.
Combine pepper and onion mixture, rice, and next 4 ingredients. Spoon about 1 cup mixture onto half of each tortilla; top evenly with sour cream and cheese. Fold tortillas in half.
Yield: 4 servings (serving size: 1 taco).

Per Serving: Calories **354** Fat **5.8g** (sat **1.9g**) Protein **15.3g** Carbohydrate **58.7g** Fiber **5.7g**
Cholesterol **8mg** Iron **3.8mg** Sodium **399mg** Calcium **93mg**
Exchanges: 4 Starch, 1 Fat

15-Minute Chili

prep: 5 minutes   cook: 10 minutes

This hearty chili is one of the easiest—and tastiest—around. Hot beans, salsa, and chili powder provide the heat, while tomatoes, peppers, and corn add garden-fresh appeal. For even more heat, add a small amount of chopped fresh pepper such as habanero, jalapeño, banana, serrano, or Scotch bonnet.

1   (16-ounce) can chili hot beans, undrained
1   (15-ounce) can black beans, rinsed and drained
1   (14.5-ounce) can Mexican-style stewed tomatoes with jalapeño
        peppers and spices, undrained
1   cup frozen whole-kernel corn
½   cup chunky salsa
1   tablespoon ground cumin
2   teaspoons chili powder
1   cup frozen chopped green bell pepper
¼   cup fat-free sour cream
¼   cup (1 ounce) preshredded reduced-fat Cheddar cheese

Combine first 8 ingredients in a large saucepan; cover. Bring to a boil. Reduce heat; simmer 10 minutes, stirring occasionally. Ladle chili into each of 4 bowls; top each serving with 1 tablespoon sour cream and 1 tablespoon cheese.

Yield: 4 servings (serving size: 1½ cups).

Per Serving: Calories **290**   Fat **3.9g** (sat **1.4g**)   Protein **16.7g**   Carbohydrate **48.9g**   Fiber **11.1g**
Cholesterol **5mg**   Iron **4.2mg**   Sodium **908mg**   Calcium **139mg**
Exchanges: 2 Starch, 2 Vegetable, ½ Fat

Pasta with Asparagus and Walnuts

prep: 1 minute   cook: 7 minutes   stand: 5 minutes

To toast the walnuts, place a heavy skillet over high heat. Add the nuts, and cook 1 to 2 minutes, stirring often, until the nuts are toasted.

1   (4.7-ounce) package angel hair pasta with butter and garlic
    (Pasta Roni)
2   cups water
½   cup coarsely chopped sun-dried tomatoes, packed without oil
¾   pound asparagus spears
¼   cup chopped walnuts, toasted

Cook pasta according to package directions, using 2 cups water and omitting milk and fat. Stir sun-dried tomatoes into water with pasta.
While pasta cooks, snap off tough ends of asparagus. Remove scales with a vegetable peeler, if desired. Cut asparagus into 1-inch pieces. Add asparagus to pasta the last 2 minutes of cooking time. Drain well.
Add walnuts to pasta mixture, and toss gently. Let stand 5 minutes before serving.
Yield: 3 servings (serving size: 1½ cups).

Per Serving: Calories **306** Fat **7.9g** (sat **1.1g**) Protein **12.2g** Carbohydrate **49.0g** Fiber **5.7g** Cholesterol **0mg** Iron **1.3mg** Sodium **674mg** Calcium **29mg**
Exchanges: 3 Starch, 1 Vegetable, 2 Fat

• vegetarian •

Pasta Primavera

prep: 4 minutes   cook: 8 minutes

*Soft breadsticks and fresh melon are the perfect complements to this
one-dish meal.*

1   (9-ounce) package refrigerated fettuccine, uncooked
Cooking spray
1   cup broccoli florets
1   cup sliced carrot
1¼ cups thinly sliced zucchini (about 1 small)
1   cup sliced mushrooms
2   garlic cloves, minced
1   (10-ounce) container refrigerated light Alfredo sauce (such as
      Contadina)
2   tablespoons chopped fresh basil
½   teaspoon freshly ground black pepper
¼   teaspoon salt
¼   cup freshly grated Parmesan cheese

Cook pasta according to package directions, omitting salt and fat;
drain, and keep warm.
While pasta cooks, heat a large nonstick skillet coated with cooking
spray over medium-high heat. Add broccoli and carrot; sauté 3 to 5
minutes or until tender. Add zucchini, mushrooms, and garlic; sauté
5 minutes or until tender. Add Alfredo sauce and next 3 ingredients
to vegetable mixture; cook until thoroughly heated.
Pour sauce mixture over pasta; toss well. Sprinkle with cheese.
Serve immediately.
Yield: 4 servings (serving size: 1½ cups).

Per Serving: Calories 334   Fat **9.8g** (sat **6.0g**)   Protein **16.2g**   Carbohydrate **47.1g**   Fiber **3.3g**
Cholesterol **90mg**   Iron **2.2mg**   Sodium **696mg**   Calcium **231mg**
Exchanges: 3 Starch, 1 Vegetable, 1 Medium-Fat Meat

Linguine with Vegetables and Asiago Cheese *(photo, page 11)*

prep: 5 minutes   cook: 10 minutes

Our Caesar Salad (recipe on page 205), warm, crusty Italian rolls, and this creamy pasta make an ideal menu for last-minute entertaining.

8   ounces uncooked linguine or fettuccine
¾   cup vegetable broth
1   (16-ounce) package fresh broccoli, cauliflower, and carrot medley
½   (10-ounce) container refrigerated light Alfredo sauce (such as
      Contadina)
½   cup freshly shredded Asiago or Parmesan cheese
Freshly ground black pepper

Cook pasta according to package directions, omitting salt and fat.
While pasta cooks, combine broth and vegetables in a medium saucepan over low heat. Cover and simmer 5 minutes or until vegetables are crisp-tender. Add Alfredo sauce, stirring well.
Drain pasta, and place in a serving bowl. Add vegetable mixture, and toss to coat; top with cheese, and sprinkle with pepper.
Yield: 4 servings (serving size: 1¾ cups).

Per Serving: Calories **341**   Fat **6.9g** (sat **3.7g**)   Protein **16.7g**   Carbohydrate **53.5g**   Fiber **4.4g**
Cholesterol **19mg**   Iron **2.6mg**   Sodium **550mg**   Calcium **283mg**
Exchanges: 3 Starch, 2 Vegetable, 1 Medium-Fat Meat

Chili Mac

prep: 3 minutes   cook: 15 minutes

If you're watching your sodium intake, check the ingredient label on the chili powder container. Some brands add more salt than others.

1½   cups uncooked elbow macaroni
1   (15-ounce) can vegetarian chili with beans (such as Hormel)
1   (16-ounce) can dark red kidney beans, rinsed and drained
½   teaspoon chili powder
¾   cup (3 ounces) preshredded reduced-fat sharp Cheddar cheese
½   cup fat-free sour cream
Additional chili powder (optional)

Cook macaroni according to package directions, omitting salt and fat. Drain well, and set aside.
Combine chili, kidney beans, and chili powder in a large nonstick skillet; add macaroni. Cook over medium heat 5 minutes or until hot, stirring often. Spoon into serving bowls; sprinkle with cheese, and top evenly with sour cream. Sprinkle additional chili powder over sour cream, if desired.
Yield: 6 servings (serving size: about 1 cup).

Per Serving: Calories **369**   Fat **3.4g** (sat **1.7g**)   Protein **22.0g**   Carbohydrate **61.9g**   Fiber **8.6g**
Cholesterol **9mg**   Iron **2.7mg**   Sodium **776mg**   Calcium **146mg**
Exchanges: 4 Starch, 1 Vegetable, 1 Lean Meat

Creamy Macaroni and Cheese

prep: 3 minutes   cook: 13 minutes   stand: 2 minutes

For a well-balanced meal, serve this family favorite with steamed carrots and a broccoli salad.

3   cups uncooked elbow macaroni
1   (10¾-ounce) can 98%-fat-free cream of mushroom soup
1   cup (4 ounces) processed cheese (such as Velveeta), cubed
1   (12-ounce) can evaporated fat-free milk
Butter-flavored cooking spray
½   cup (2 ounces) preshredded reduced-fat sharp Cheddar cheese or
        Swiss cheese
¼   cup dry breadcrumbs
½   teaspoon paprika

Cook macaroni according to package directions, omitting salt and fat; drain. (Do not rinse.)
While macaroni cooks, combine soup, cheese cubes, and milk in a heavy saucepan over medium heat, stirring constantly until cheese melts. (Do not boil.)
Coat an 11 x 7-inch microwave-safe baking dish with cooking spray. Add macaroni. Pour cheese mixture over macaroni, and stir gently. Sprinkle with shredded Cheddar cheese; top with breadcrumbs, and sprinkle with paprika. Lightly coat breadcrumbs with cooking spray. Microwave at HIGH, uncovered, 5 minutes. Let stand 2 minutes before serving.
Yield: 6 servings (serving size: about 1⅓ cups).

Per Serving: Calories **323**   Fat **7.8g** (sat **3.9g**)   Protein **15.9g**   Carbohydrate **45.7g**   Fiber **1.0g**
Cholesterol **23mg**   Iron **2.1mg**   Sodium **675mg**   Calcium **384mg**
Exchanges: 3 Starch, 1 Medium-Fat Meat

Mostaccioli with Red Pepper Sauce

prep: 5 minutes   cook: 10 minutes

Substitute rigatoni or penne pasta for mostaccioli. Serve with a tossed green salad.

8   ounces uncooked mostaccioli (tube-shaped pasta)
2   cups sliced zucchini (about 2 medium)
1   garlic clove
1   (7-ounce) bottle roasted red bell peppers, drained
1   tablespoon balsamic vinegar
¼   cup fat-free mayonnaise
3   tablespoons grated Parmesan cheese
Chopped fresh basil (optional)

Cook pasta according to package directions, omitting salt and fat. Add zucchini, and cook 2 minutes or until zucchini is tender.
While pasta and zucchini cook, drop garlic though food chute with food processor on; process until garlic is finely chopped. Add peppers and vinegar to processor; process 1 minute, stopping once to scrape down sides. Add mayonnaise and cheese; process just until combined.
Drain pasta-zucchini mixture; transfer to a large bowl. Add red pepper sauce to pasta, and toss gently. Garnish with chopped fresh basil, if desired.
Yield: 4 servings (serving size: about 1½ cups).

Per Serving: Calories **262** Fat **2.3g** (sat **0.9g**) Protein **10.1g** Carbohydrate **50.3g** Fiber **2.2g**
Cholesterol **3mg** Iron **2.8mg** Sodium **269mg** Calcium **80mg**
Exchanges: 3 Starch, 1 Vegetable

• vegetarian •

Penne with White Beans

prep: 3 minutes   cook: 8 minutes

Chop the basil while the pasta cooks. The chopping is faster when you arrange the leaves in a stack, and chop with a sharp knife. Serve with fresh tomato slices and garlic breadsticks.

8   ounces uncooked penne (tube-shaped pasta)
2   (16-ounce) cans cannellini beans or other white beans, rinsed and
        drained
1   (7-ounce) bottle roasted red bell peppers, drained and chopped
½   cup chopped fresh basil
¼   cup balsamic vinegar
1   tablespoon olive oil
½   teaspoon salt
½   teaspoon freshly ground black pepper
⅓   cup (about 2 ounces) crumbled feta cheese with basil and
        sun-dried tomatoes

Cook pasta according to package directions, omitting salt and fat. Drain and return pasta to saucepan.
Add beans and next 6 ingredients to saucepan; toss gently. Spoon mixture onto serving plates, and sprinkle evenly with feta. Serve immediately.
Yield: 7 servings (serving size: about 1⅓ cups).

Per Serving: Calories **273**   Fat **7.5g** (sat **3.4g**)   Protein **12.1g**   Carbohydrate **37.6g**   Fiber **5.1g**
Cholesterol **15mg**   Iron **2.8mg**   Sodium **723mg**   Calcium **29mg**
Exchanges: 2 Starch, 2 Vegetable, 1½ Fat

Cheese Ravioli with Tomatoes and Peppers

prep: 5 minutes   cook: 7 minutes

Serve with warm Italian bread sprinkled with garlic powder. For dessert, prepare Double Berry-Brownie Dessert (recipe on page 71).

1   (9-ounce) package refrigerated cheese-filled ravioli, uncooked
1   teaspoon olive oil
1   medium green bell pepper, cut into thin strips
1   medium onion, cut into thin strips
2   teaspoons minced garlic
3   cups chopped tomato (3 medium)
¾   teaspoon freshly ground black pepper
1   cup loosely packed fresh basil leaves, slivered

Cook pasta according to package directions.
While pasta cooks, heat oil in a large nonstick skillet over medium-high heat. Add green bell pepper, onion, and garlic; cook 3 minutes or until vegetables begin to wilt. Stir in tomato, and cook 2 minutes or until tomatoes are soft. Stir in ground pepper and basil; remove from heat.
Drain pasta, and place in a large serving bowl; pour sauce over pasta. Serve immediately.
Yield: 3 servings (serving size: 1½ cups).

Per Serving: Calories **362** Fat **11.2g** (sat **5.3g**) Protein **16.3g** Carbohydrate **50.8g** Fiber **6.3g**
Cholesterol **70mg** Iron **2.4mg** Sodium **356mg** Calcium **226mg**
Exchanges: 3 Starch, 1 Vegetable, 1 Medium-Fat Meat

Vegetarian Peanut Pasta

prep: 5 minutes   cook: 10 minutes

You can substitute 1½ cups broccoli florets for snow peas in this pasta recipe—just cook as directed in step two. For a bit of crunch, sprinkle each serving with 2 teaspoons chopped dry-roasted peanuts. Serve with warmed bread rounds, fresh orange wedges, and sliced bananas.

¼   cup plus 2 tablespoons reduced-fat peanut butter
¼   cup plus 1½ teaspoons water
3   tablespoons brown sugar
3   tablespoons low-sodium soy sauce
3   tablespoons rice vinegar
¼   to ½ teaspoon dried crushed red pepper
8   ounces uncooked spaghetti
10 ounces snow peas, trimmed
1   large carrot, shredded

Combine first 6 ingredients in a small saucepan. Cook over medium heat until mixture begins to boil, stirring often; remove from heat, and set sauce aside.

While sauce cooks, cook pasta according to package directions, omitting salt and fat; add snow peas to pasta the last 3 minutes of cooking time. Drain and place in a large serving bowl. Add carrot and sauce, tossing to coat. Serve immediately.

Yield: 5 servings (serving size: about 1⅔ cups).

Per Serving: Calories **339**   Fat **8.1g** (sat **0.1g**)   Protein **12.3g**   Carbohydrate **54.2g**   Fiber **4.3g**
Cholesterol **0mg**   Iron **4.9mg**   Sodium **398mg**   Calcium **57mg**
Exchanges: 3 Starch, 1 Vegetable, 1 Medium-Fat Meat

Hearty Spaghetti

prep: 1 minute   cook: 16 minutes

Toss fresh apple slices, creamy light ranch-style dressing, and romaine lettuce together for a salad. Lightly spray slices of Italian bread with butter-flavored cooking spray, and toast them until golden.

12 ounces uncooked spaghetti
Cooking spray
1   teaspoon bottled minced garlic
1   (10-ounce) package frozen chopped onion
1   (8-ounce) package presliced mushrooms
1   (14.5-ounce) can no-salt-added stewed tomatoes, undrained
1   (6-ounce) can tomato paste
1   cup water
1   (12-ounce) package all-vegetable burger crumbles
¼   teaspoon salt
1   tablespoon dried Italian seasoning

Cook pasta according to package directions, omitting salt and fat; drain and keep warm.
While pasta cooks, coat a Dutch oven with cooking spray; place over medium-high heat until hot. Add garlic, onion, and mushrooms; cook 5 minutes or until liquid is absorbed, stirring occasionally.
Reduce heat to medium; add tomatoes, tomato paste, and water. Cook 1 minute, stirring well. Add vegetable crumbles, salt, and Italian seasoning. Cover, reduce heat to medium-low, and simmer 10 minutes, stirring once. To serve, spoon tomato mixture evenly over 1 cup portions of cooked pasta.
Yield: 6 servings.

Per Serving: Calories **349** Fat **1.6g** (sat **0.2g**) Protein **20.7g** Carbohydrate **63.6g** Fiber **6.3g**
Cholesterol **0mg** Iron **5.9mg** Sodium **396mg** Calcium **95mg**
Exchanges: 3½ Starch, 2 Vegetable

Mediterranean Pasta

prep: 7 minutes   cook: 7 minutes

Look for fresh pasta in the refrigerated section of the supermarket.
Serve with a tossed green salad and breadsticks.

1   (9-ounce) package fresh cheese tortellini, uncooked
1   (16-ounce) jar fat-free marinara sauce (about 2 cups)
1   (14-ounce) can quartered artichoke hearts, drained and coarsely
      chopped
3   tablespoons chopped ripe olives
2   tablespoons grated Parmesan cheese
2   tablespoons dry breadcrumbs
½   teaspoon dried Italian seasoning

Preheat broiler.
Cook pasta according to package directions, omitting salt and fat;
drain.
While pasta cooks, place marinara sauce in a small saucepan, and
cook over medium heat 4 to 5 minutes or until thoroughly heated,
stirring occasionally.
Combine tortellini, sauce, artichokes, and olives in a 1½-quart casserole
dish. Combine cheese, breadcrumbs, and seasoning; sprinkle over pasta
mixture. Broil 2 minutes or until lightly browned.
Yield: 5 servings (serving size: about 1 cup).

Per Serving: Calories **253** Fat **4.1g** (sat **2.9g**) Protein **12.3g** Carbohydrate **38.6g** Fiber **1.5g**
Cholesterol **34mg** Iron **1.2mg** Sodium **811mg** Calcium **104mg**
Exchanges: 2 Starch, 2 Vegetable, 1 Fat

• vegetarian •

Curried Vegetable Couscous

prep: 4 minutes   cook: 11 minutes

Couscous, made from wheat, fluffs up like rice when it's cooked. The best part is that it takes only five minutes to prepare. Find couscous in the rice and pasta section of your supermarket.

1   (14½-ounce) can vegetable broth, divided
⅓   cup raisins
1   cup uncooked couscous
½   (16-ounce) package fresh stir-fry vegetables
¼   cup water
2   teaspoons curry powder
¼   teaspoon ground red pepper
1   (15.8-ounce) can black-eyed peas, rinsed and drained

Combine 1¼ cups broth and raisins in a small saucepan. Bring to a boil, and stir in couscous. Cover, remove from heat, and let stand 5 minutes.

While couscous stands, combine remaining broth, stir-fry vegetables, and remaining 4 ingredients in a saucepan; stir well. Cover and simmer 7 minutes or until vegetables are crisp-tender. Serve over couscous mixture.

Yield: 4 servings.

Per Serving: Calories **293** Fat **1.6g** (sat **0.2g**) Protein **13.2g** Carbohydrate **58.6g** Fiber **5.2g**
Cholesterol **0mg** Iron **2.5mg** Sodium **364mg** Calcium **35mg**
Exchanges: 2 Starch, 1 Fruit, 2 Vegetable

meatless main dishes | **143**

Couscous with Italian Vegetable Ragoût

prep: 5 minutes   cook: 15 minutes

One (10-ounce) package of couscous makes 5 cups of cooked couscous, so be sure to buy two packages for this recipe. Prepare the couscous while the vegetable mixture simmers.

4   cups thinly sliced zucchini (about 4 small)
2   cups coarsely chopped onion (about 1 medium)
2   (14½-ounce) cans Italian-style stewed tomatoes, undrained
1   (15-ounce) can no-salt-added chickpeas (garbanzo beans), rinsed
        and drained
1   teaspoon dried Italian seasoning
¼   teaspoon salt
¼   teaspoon freshly ground black pepper
7   cups cooked couscous

Combine first 7 ingredients in a large skillet. Bring to a boil; cover, reduce heat, and simmer 10 minutes, stirring occasionally. Uncover and simmer 5 minutes or until most of liquid evaporates.

Arrange 1 cup couscous on each of 7 serving plates; top each evenly with vegetable mixture.

Yield: 7 servings.

Per Serving: Calories **295**   Fat **1.4g** (sat **0.1g**)   Protein **11.2g**   Carbohydrate **61.6g**   Fiber **5.9g**
Cholesterol **0mg**   Iron **2.8mg**   Sodium **503mg**   Calcium **73mg**
Exchanges: 3 Starch, 2 Vegetable

• vegetarian •

Herbed Polenta with Portobellos

prep: 2 minutes   cook: 13 minutes

Packages of polenta are located in the produce section of your super-market. The package shape is similar to that of ground sausage. Serve with a spinach salad and whole wheat rolls.

Olive oil-flavored cooking spray
1 (16-ounce) tube Italian herb or plain polenta
½ cup (2 ounces) grated fresh Asiago or Parmesan cheese, divided
1 (6-ounce) package presliced portobello mushrooms
½ cup sliced onion (about 1 small)
¼ cup red wine
¼ cup vegetable broth
¼ to ½ teaspoon dried rosemary, crushed

Heat a large skillet coated with cooking spray over high heat. While pan heats, cut polenta into 9 slices. Add polenta slices to pan, and cook 4 minutes on each side or until lightly browned.

Remove pan from heat, and transfer polenta slices to a warm serving platter. While polenta is hot, sprinkle slices with half of cheese. Cover and keep warm.

Wipe same pan with paper towels, and coat with cooking spray; place over medium-high heat until hot. Add mushrooms and onion, and cook 4 minutes or until onion is crisp-tender, stirring often. Add wine, broth, and rosemary. Cook over high heat 1 minute or until most of liquid evaporates.

Spoon mushroom mixture evenly over polenta slices; sprinkle with remaining cheese. Serve immediately.

Yield: 3 servings (serving size: 3 polenta slices and about 1 cup mushroom mixture).

Per Serving: Calories **200**   Fat **5.7g** (sat **3.3g**)   Protein **9.6g**   Carbohydrate **27.1g**   Fiber **3.0g**
Cholesterol **17mg**   Iron **0.1mg**   Sodium **350mg**   Calcium **7mg**
Exchanges: 1 Starch, 2 Vegetable, 1 Fat

Sweet-and-Sour Tofu Stir-Fry

prep: 5 minutes   cook: 10 minutes

To keep from crumbling, stir the tofu gently while it cooks. Serve with fresh orange slices and fortune cookies.

1   extralarge bag quick-cooking boil-in-bag rice
Cooking spray
1   teaspoon sesame oil
1   (12.3-ounce) package firm tofu, drained and cubed
1   (21-ounce) package frozen sweet and sour stir-fry, thawed
2   tablespoons low-sodium soy sauce

Cook rice according to package directions, omitting salt and fat.
While rice cooks, coat a wok or large skillet with cooking spray; add oil. Place over medium-high heat until hot. Add tofu, and cook 4 to 5 minutes or until tofu is lightly browned, stirring often. Remove tofu, and drain.
Add sauce from stir-fry mix to wok, and cook 1 minute. Add vegetables; cover and cook 5 minutes or until vegetables are tender. Stir in soy sauce. Add tofu, stirring gently. To serve, spoon tofu mixture evenly over 1-cup portions of rice.
Yield: 3 servings.

Per Serving: Calories **309**   Fat **6.4g** (sat **0.9g**)   Protein **12.6g**   Carbohydrate **50.8g**   Fiber **5.8g**
Cholesterol **0mg**   Iron **6.1mg**   Sodium **654mg**   Calcium **111mg**
Exchanges: 3 Starch, 1 Vegetable, 1 Fat

meats

Peppery Mushroom Burgers

prep: 5 minutes   cook: 13 minutes

Patties thicker than ¼ inch will take longer to cook. Serve with New Potatoes in Seasoned Butter (recipe on page 233) and steamed green beans.

1   (8-ounce) package presliced mushrooms, divided
1   pound ground round
2   teaspoons instant minced onion
2   teaspoons low-sodium Worcestershire sauce
1   teaspoon freshly ground black pepper
Cooking spray
¼   cup dry red wine or no-salt-added beef broth
¼   cup water

Coarsely chop 1½ cups sliced mushrooms. Combine beef, chopped mushrooms, onion, and Worcestershire sauce in a bowl; shape into 4 equal patties, ¼ inch thick. Sprinkle pepper evenly on both sides of patties.

Heat a 12-inch nonstick skillet coated with cooking spray over medium-high heat. Add patties, and cook 5 to 6 minutes on each side or until done. Transfer to a serving platter, and keep warm.

Add wine, water, and remaining mushrooms to pan; cook over medium heat, stirring constantly, scraping pan to loosen browned bits about 3 minutes or until mushrooms are tender. Pour mushroom mixture evenly over patties.

Yield: 4 servings.

Per Serving: Calories **181**   Fat **6.0g** (sat **2.1g**)   Protein **26.3g**   Carbohydrate **4.4g**   Fiber **0.9g**
Cholesterol **66mg**   Iron **3.4mg**   Sodium **78mg**   Calcium **13mg**
Exchanges: 1 Vegetable, 3 Lean Meat

Beef Patties with Sweet-and-Sour Onions

prep: 5 minutes   cook: 10 minutes

It's important to thaw the frozen onion, and then drain it well so the saucy gravy won't be watered down and thin. Serve with rice, steamed green and red bell peppers, and soft dinner rolls.

1   pound ground round
¼   teaspoon garlic powder
¼   teaspoon freshly ground black pepper
Olive oil-flavored cooking spray
1   (12-ounce) package frozen chopped onion (about 2½ cups)
2   tablespoons sugar
2   tablespoons balsamic vinegar

Combine first 3 ingredients; stir well. Shape meat mixture into 4 equal patties, ¼ inch thick.

Heat a large nonstick skillet coated with cooking spray over medium-high heat. Place patties in pan, and cook 5 minutes on each side or until done.

While patties cook, thaw onion by placing in a strainer or colander under warm running water. Drain well. Transfer patties to a serving platter, and keep warm. Add onion, sugar, and vinegar to pan; cook 4 minutes over medium heat or until onion mixture is slightly thickened. Pour onion mixture evenly over patties, and serve immediately.

Yield: 4 servings.

Per Serving: Calories **226**   Fat **5.9g** (sat **2.1g**)   Protein **26.3g**   Carbohydrate **15.6g**   Fiber **2.0g**
Cholesterol **66mg**   Iron **2.7mg**   Sodium **68mg**   Calcium **27mg**
Exchanges: 1 Starch, 3 Lean Meat

South-of-the-Border Pizzas

prep: 15 minutes   cook: 9 minutes

Go light with these tortilla pizzas, a tossed green salad drizzled with fat-free Italian dressing, and fresh pineapple slices.

3   (10-inch) flour tortillas
½   pound ground round
1   (15-ounce) can no-salt-added black beans, rinsed and drained
1   (1.25-ounce) package reduced-sodium taco seasoning
¼   cup water
2   large tomatoes, finely chopped
½   cup sliced green onions (about 4)
2   tablespoons chopped fresh cilantro
1   tablespoon minced jalapeño pepper
1   cup preshredded reduced-fat Mexican cheese blend or Cheddar
        cheese

Preheat oven to 450°.

Place tortillas on two baking sheets, and bake at 450° for 2 minutes or until slightly crisp.

While tortillas bake, cook ground round in a nonstick skillet over medium heat until browned, stirring until it crumbles. Drain and pat dry with paper towels; return to pan. Add beans, taco seasoning, and water; bring to a boil. Reduce heat to low, and simmer 3 minutes, stirring often.

Spread beef mixture over tortillas, leaving a ½-inch border. Combine tomato and next 3 ingredients; sprinkle over beef mixture. Top with cheese.

Bake at 450° for 4 minutes or until cheese melts and tortillas are lightly browned. Remove pizzas to a cutting board; let stand 5 minutes before cutting each pizza in half.

Yield: 6 servings (serving size: ½ pizza).

Per Serving: Calories **300** Fat **7.6g** (sat **3.2g**) Protein **21.6g** Carbohydrate **40.4g** Fiber **6.2g**
Cholesterol **30mg** Iron **3.0mg** Sodium **641mg** Calcium **227mg**
Exchanges: 1½ Starch, 1 Vegetable, 3 Lean Meat

Sante Fe Skillet Hamburger Casserole

prep: 5 minutes   cook: 15 minutes

Serve with steamed green beans and Pineapple-Mint Ice (recipe on page 88).

1   pound ground round
¾   cup chopped onion (1 small)
¾   cup chopped green bell pepper (1 medium)
1½   cups instant rice, uncooked
1½   cups no-salt-added beef broth
¼   teaspoon salt
¼   teaspoon black pepper
1   (14.5-ounce) can Mexican-style stewed tomatoes with jalapeño
        peppers and spices, undrained
¾   cup (3 ounces) preshredded reduced-fat sharp Cheddar cheese

Combine first 3 ingredients in a large nonstick skillet; cook over medium-high heat until beef is browned and vegetables are tender, stirring until beef crumbles. (Do not drain.)
Add rice and next 4 ingredients. Cover, reduce heat, and simmer 5 minutes or until rice is tender and liquid is absorbed. Sprinkle with cheese; serve immediately.
Yield: 6 servings.

Per Serving: Calories **346**   Fat **15.8g** (sat **6.8g**)   Protein **21.1g**   Carbohydrate **28.5g**   Fiber **2.1g**
Cholesterol **62mg**   Iron **2.9mg**   Sodium **488mg**   Calcium **152mg**
Exchanges: 1½ Starch, 1 Vegetable, 3 Medium-Fat Meat

Spaghetti with Beef, Tomatoes, and Zucchini

prep: 5 minutes   cook: 12 minutes

Serve with freshly sliced melon, such as cantaloupe and honeydew, and lemon fat-free frozen yogurt.

1   (7-ounce) package thin spaghetti
½   pound ground round
¼   cup chopped onion (½ small)
2   (8-ounce) cans no-salt-added tomato sauce
1   teaspoon dried Italian seasoning
½   teaspoon salt
¼   teaspoon garlic powder
¼   teaspoon dried crushed red pepper
1½ cups coarsely chopped zucchini (about 1 medium)
1½ cups coarsely chopped tomato (about 1 medium)

Cook spaghetti according to package directions, omitting salt and fat.
While spaghetti cooks, cook ground round and onion in a large nonstick skillet over high heat 4 to 5 minutes or until beef is browned, stirring until beef crumbles. Drain beef mixture, if necessary; wipe pan with paper towels. Return beef mixture to pan. Stir in tomato sauce and next 4 ingredients. Cook over medium heat 2 to 4 minutes or until hot and bubbly, stirring occasionally.
Stir in cooked spaghetti and zucchini. Cook 2 minutes, stirring occasionally. Stir in tomato.
Yield: 4 servings (serving size: 1½ cups).

Per Serving: Calories 332 Fat **7.9g** (sat **2.9g**) Protein **19.3g** Carbohydrate **46.4g** Fiber **2.2g**
Cholesterol **35mg** Iron **3.7mg** Sodium **336mg** Calcium **33mg**
Exchanges: 2 Starch, 2 Vegetable, 2 Lean Meat

Teriyaki Flank Steak

prep: 5 minutes   cook: 10 minutes

Use a sharp knife or an electric knife to slice the steak into very thin slices. Serve with brown rice and steamed snow peas.

1   (1-pound) lean flank steak (½ inch thick), trimmed
¼   cup honey
¼   cup low-sodium soy sauce
1   teaspoon ground ginger
1   teaspoon sesame oil
½   teaspoon minced garlic (1 clove)
¼   teaspoon salt
¼   teaspoon freshly ground black pepper
Cooking spray

Prepare grill.
Place flank steak in a large heavy-duty, zip-top plastic bag. Combine honey and next 6 ingredients; stir well. Pour marinade over steak; seal bag securely. Turn bag to coat steak.
While grill heats, remove steak from marinade, reserving marinade. Place marinade in a small saucepan; bring to a boil, and cook 1 minute. Remove from heat, and set aside.
Place steak on grill rack coated with cooking spray; cover and grill 5 to 6 minutes on each side or until steak is done, basting occasionally with marinade. Cut steak diagonally across grain into ¼-inch-thick slices.
Yield: 4 servings.

Per Serving: Calories **237** Fat **13.0g** (sat **5.5g**) Protein **22.0g** Carbohydrate **7.2g** Fiber **0.0g**
Cholesterol **60mg** Iron **2.3mg** Sodium **366mg** Calcium **7mg**
Exchanges: ½ Starch, 3 Medium-Fat Meat

Mexican Cubed Steaks

prep: 2 minutes   cook: 14 minutes

Cubed steak is simply a steak that has been rolled through a machine that punches holes in the meat to tenderize it. If you don't see cubed steaks prepackaged at the meat counter, ask the butcher to cube some steaks for you. Serve with rice, black beans, and fresh pineapple wedges.

Cooking spray
1   teaspoon vegetable oil
4   (4-ounce) cubed steaks
1   (8-ounce) jar picante sauce
2   tablespoons lime juice
¼   teaspoon freshly ground black pepper
¼   cup chopped fresh cilantro or parsley

Coat a large nonstick skillet with cooking spray; add oil. Place over medium-high heat until hot. Add steaks; cook 2 minutes on each side. **Combine** picante sauce, lime juice, and pepper; pour over steaks. Cover, reduce heat, and simmer 10 minutes. Sprinkle with cilantro.
Yield: 4 servings.

Per Serving: Calories **225**   Fat **7.0g** (sat **2.3g**)   Protein **27.9g**   Carbohydrate **12.1g**   Fiber **1.6g**
Cholesterol **69mg**   Iron **3.2mg**   Sodium **929mg**   Calcium **11mg**
Exchanges: 1 Starch, 3 Lean Meat

Gingered Beef Stir-Fry

prep: 5 minutes   cook: 5 minutes

You can substitute snow peas or zucchini strips for sugar snap peas.
Serve with rice and steamed yellow squash.

½   cup no-salt-added beef broth
1   tablespoon low-sodium soy sauce
1   teaspoon cornstarch
1   teaspoon ground ginger
¼   to ½ teaspoon dried crushed red pepper
Cooking spray
1   teaspoon dark sesame oil
½   pound boneless sirloin steak, cut crosswise into
        ¼-inch-thick strips
1   (8-ounce) package frozen sugar snap peas

Combine first 5 ingredients; stir well.
Coat a wok or large nonstick skillet with cooking spray; drizzle oil
around top of wok, coating sides. Heat at medium-high until hot. Add
steak, and stir-fry 2 minutes or until lightly browned.
Add peas and broth mixture to wok; stir-fry 3 minutes or until thickened.
Yield: 2 servings.

Per Serving: Calories **249**   Fat **8.7g** (sat **2.5g**)   Protein **28.8g**   Carbohydrate **12.1g**   Fiber **3.7g**
Cholesterol **69mg**   Iron **5.8mg**   Sodium **316mg**   Calcium **64mg**
Exchanges: 1 Starch, 3 Lean Meat

Barbecued Steak Pizza

prep: 2 minutes   cook: 13 minutes

Serve with a salad made of fresh spinach, sliced red onion, and mandarin orange sections; drizzle fat-free poppy seed dressing over the salad.

1   (1-pound) boneless sirloin steak
½   cup barbecue sauce
1   (10-ounce) Italian cheese-flavored thin pizza crust (such as Boboli)
Cooking spray
½   cup onion strips (about 1 small)
½   cup green bell pepper strips (1 small)
½   cup (2 ounces) preshredded reduced-fat Cheddar cheese

Prepare grill.

Brush both sides of steak with barbecue sauce. Brush remaining sauce over pizza crust. Place steak on grill rack coated with cooking spray; grill 5 to 6 minutes on each side or until steak is done.

While steak grills, heat a large nonstick skillet coated with cooking spray over medium-high heat. Add onion and bell pepper; cook 3 minutes or until crisp-tender, stirring often. Spoon vegetables over pizza crust.

Preheat broiler.

Arrange beef in a spiral pattern over vegetables, and sprinkle with cheese. Broil 3 to 4 minutes or until cheese melts.

Yield: 6 servings (serving size: 1 slice).

Per Serving: Calories **291**   Fat **9.5g** (sat **2.8g**)   Protein **27.3g**   Carbohydrate **23.3g**   Fiber **0.4g**
Cholesterol **64mg**   Iron **2.4mg**   Sodium **520mg**   Calcium **96mg**
Exchanges: 1 Starch, 1 Vegetable, 3 Lean Meat

Chili-Rubbed Sirloin with Corn-Bean Salsa

prep: 2 minutes   cook: 12 minutes

Serve with a tossed green salad. For dessert, we suggest Citrusy Melon and Strawberry Cup (recipe on page 81).

1	tablespoon chili powder
1	teaspoon ground cumin
½	teaspoon ground red pepper
1	(1-pound) boneless sirloin steak (1 inch thick)

Cooking spray

½	cup thick and chunky cilantro-flavored salsa
1	cup frozen whole-kernel corn, thawed
1	cup drained canned no-salt-added pinto beans
½	cup sliced green onions (2 large)

Prepare grill.

Combine first 3 ingredients in a small bowl; rub evenly over steak, pressing onto steak.

Place steak on grill rack coated with cooking spray; cover and grill 6 minutes on each side or until steak is done.

While steak grills, combine salsa and remaining 3 ingredients.

Cut steak diagonally across grain into ¼-inch-thick slices. Top with salsa mixture.

Yield: 4 servings (serving size: 3 ounces steak and about ¾ cup salsa).

Per Serving: Calories **283** Fat **7.5g** (sat **2.6g**) Protein **32.4g** Carbohydrate **22.6g** Fiber **4.0g**
Cholesterol **80mg** Iron **4.2mg** Sodium **240mg** Calcium **38mg**
Exchanges: 1½ Starch, 3 Lean Meat

Chuckwagon Steak
with Chili Rub

prep: 6 minutes   cook: 10 minutes

Serve with steamed sugar snap peas and an endive salad. Dress up the endive with a splash of balsamic vinegar and a sprinkling of crumbled blue cheese.

1   (1-pound) boneless sirloin steak (about ½ inch thick)
Cooking spray
1   tablespoon chili powder
2   teaspoons coarsely ground black pepper
½   teaspoon salt
4   garlic cloves, minced

Prepare grill.
Coat both sides of steak with cooking spray. Combine chili powder and remaining 3 ingredients; rub on both sides of steak.
Place steak on grill rack coated with cooking spray; cover and grill 5 minutes on each side or until steak is done. Cut diagonally across grain into thin slices.
Yield: 4 servings.

Per Serving: Calories **189**   Fat **7.0g** (sat **2.6g**)   Protein **27.7g**   Carbohydrate **2.7g**   Fiber **1.0g**
Cholesterol **80mg**   Iron **3.6mg**   Sodium **372mg**   Calcium **25mg**
Exchanges: 3 Lean Meat

Sirloin Steak with Garlic Sauce

prep: 5 minutes   cook: 10 minutes

Roast extra cloves of garlic, and freeze them for later. Serve with mashed potatoes and steamed broccoli.

1   (1-pound) boneless sirloin steak (1 inch thick), well-trimmed
1   teaspoon dried thyme
¼   teaspoon salt
¼   teaspoon freshly ground black pepper
Cooking spray
8   large garlic cloves, unpeeled
⅓   cup no-salt-added beef broth

Preheat broiler.

Sprinkle both sides of steak with thyme, salt, and pepper. Place steaks on a broiler pan coated with cooking spray; arrange garlic cloves around steak.

Broil steak and garlic 5 to 6 minutes on each side or until steak is done. Transfer steak to a cutting board; cover loosely with aluminum foil to keep warm.

Cut off bottom of each garlic clove, and squeeze out soft garlic into a food processor; process until smooth. Add broth; process until combined. Transfer garlic sauce to a microwave-safe dish. Microwave at HIGH 40 seconds.

Cut steak diagonally across grain into thin slices; spoon garlic sauce over steak.

Yield: 4 servings.

Per Serving: Calories **188**   Fat **6.6g** (sat **2.5g**)   Protein **27.7g**   Carbohydrate **2.5g**   Fiber **0.2g**
Cholesterol **80mg**   Iron **3.6mg**   Sodium **208mg**   Calcium **28mg**
Exchanges: 4 Very Lean Meat

Thyme-Scented Tenderloin Steaks *(photo, page 1)*

prep: 5 minutes   cook: 8 minutes

Serve with roasted potatoes and Sesame Asparagus and Mushrooms (recipe on page 226).

2   teaspoons dried thyme
2   teaspoons bottled minced garlic or 4 garlic cloves, minced
¼   teaspoon salt
¼   teaspoon freshly ground black pepper
4   (4-ounce) beef tenderloin steaks (¾ inch thick), trimmed
Cooking spray

Combine first 4 ingredients in a small bowl, and rub on both sides of steaks.
Heat a 10-inch cast iron skillet coated with cooking spray over medium heat. Add steaks; cook 4 to 6 minutes on each side or until steaks are done.
Yield: 4 servings.

Per Serving: Calories **174**   Fat **7.6g** (sat **3.0g**)   Protein **23.7g**   Carbohydrate **1.0g**   Fiber **0.2g**
Cholesterol **70mg**   Iron **4.1mg**   Sodium **208mg**   Calcium **23mg**
Exchanges: 3 Lean Meat

Peppered Filets
with Mushroom Sauce

prep: 2 minutes   cook: 10 minutes

Freshly ground pepper is more pungent and flavorful than the ground pepper in cans or jars. Serve with garlic mashed potatoes and a tossed green salad.

2   (4-ounce) beef tenderloin steaks (1 inch thick), trimmed
1   teaspoon freshly ground black pepper
Cooking spray
1   (8-ounce) package presliced mushrooms
2   green onions, sliced
¼   cup dry red wine or no-salt-added beef broth

Preheat broiler.
Sprinkle both sides of steaks evenly with pepper.
Place steaks on a broiler pan coated with cooking spray; broil 5 to 6 minutes on each side or until steak is done.
While steaks broil, heat a large nonstick skillet coated with cooking spray over medium-high heat. Add mushrooms and onions; cook 5 minutes or until mushrooms are tender. Add wine; simmer 1 minute.
Place steaks on a serving platter; spoon mushroom mixture evenly over steaks.
Yield: 2 servings.

Per Serving: Calories **211**   Fat **8.7g** (sat **3.2g**)   Protein **26.7g**   Carbohydrate **6.8g**   Fiber **1.9g**
Cholesterol **71mg**   Iron **5.0mg**   Sodium **62mg**   Calcium **23mg**
Exchanges: 1 Vegetable, 3½ Lean Meat

Rosemary-Grilled Veal Chops

prep: 4 minutes   cook: 10 minutes

Intensify the flavor of dried herbs by crushing them between your fingers or by using a mortar and pestle.

4   (6-ounce) lean veal loin chops (¾ inch thick), trimmed
Olive oil-flavored cooking spray
1½ teaspoons dried rosemary, crushed
¾   teaspoon lemon pepper seasoning

Prepare grill.
Coat both sides of veal with cooking spray. Combine rosemary and lemon pepper seasoning; rub evenly over veal.
Place veal on grill rack coated with cooking spray; cover and grill 5 to 6 minutes on each side or until veal is done.
Yield: 4 servings.

Per Serving: Calories **187** Fat **10.7g** (sat **4.5g**) Protein **21.1g** Carbohydrate **0.3g** Fiber **0.1g**
Cholesterol **88mg** Iron **0.9mg** Sodium **140mg** Calcium **21mg**
Exchanges: 3 Lean Meat

Veal Piccata

prep: 3 minutes   cook: 5 minutes

You can substitute pork medallions or boneless chicken breasts for the veal cutlets, though you may have to cook them a little longer. Be sure to flatten or pound both pork or chicken to about ¼ inch thickness. Serve with angel hair pasta and steamed asparagus.

⅓   cup dry vermouth
2   tablespoons fresh lemon juice (about 1 small lemon)
¼   teaspoon garlic powder
⅛   teaspoon salt
Butter-flavored cooking spray
½   pound veal cutlets (¼ inch thick)
2   tablespoons chopped fresh parsley

Combine first 4 ingredients, stirring well.

Heat a medium nonstick skillet coated with cooking spray over medium-high heat. Add half of veal cutlets to pan; cook 1 minute on each side. Transfer veal to a serving platter, and keep warm. Recoat pan with cooking spray, and repeat procedure with remaining veal cutlets.

Add vermouth mixture to pan. Cook over high heat 1 minute, stirring constantly, scraping pan to loosen browned bits. Pour sauce evenly over veal; sprinkle with parsley, and serve immediately.

Yield: 2 servings.

Per Serving: Calories **143**   Fat **3.6g** (sat **1.0g**)   Protein **23.1g**   Carbohydrate **3.2g**   Fiber **0.1g**
Cholesterol **94mg**   Iron **1.2mg**   Sodium **243mg**   Calcium **23mg**
Exchanges: 3 Very Lean Meat

Mint-Grilled Lamb Chops

prep: 5 minutes   cook: 10 minutes

We suggest serving the lamb chops with couscous and Maple-Glazed Apples (recipe on page 222).

⅓   cup chopped fresh mint
2   tablespoons plain low-fat yogurt
2   garlic cloves, crushed
1   small lemon, cut in half
4   (5-ounce) lamb loin chops (about 1 inch thick), trimmed
Cooking spray
Mint sprigs (optional)

Prepare grill.
Combine first 3 ingredients in a small bowl.
Place lamb on grill rack coated with cooking spray; cover and grill 5 minutes. Turn lamb; spread mint mixture evenly over lamb. Cook 5 minutes or until lamb is done. Garnish with mint sprigs, if desired.
Yield: 4 servings.

Per Serving: Calories **173**   Fat **7.9g** (sat **2.9g**)   Protein **23.0g**   Carbohydrate **1.2g**   Fiber **0.1g**
Cholesterol **74mg**   Iron **1.7mg**   Sodium **66mg**   Calcium **32mg**
Exchanges: 3 Lean Meat

Rosemary-Grilled Lamb Chops

prep: 2 minutes   cook: 12 minutes

If you have time, marinate the chops 1 to 2 hours in the refrigerator, and the chops will be even more flavorful. Serve with couscous, roasted asparagus, and crusty bread.

¼ cup balsamic vinegar
1 tablespoon lemon juice
1 tablespoon dried rosemary, crushed
¼ teaspoon garlic powder
¼ teaspoon freshly ground black pepper
Cooking spray
4 (4-ounce) lamb loin chops (about 1 inch thick), trimmed
Additional balsamic vinegar (optional)

Prepare grill.
Combine first 5 ingredients; stir well.
Place lamb on grill rack coated with cooking spray; cover and grill 6 minutes on each side or until lamb is done, basting occasionally with vinegar mixture. Serve with balsamic vinegar, if desired.

Yield: 2 servings (serving size: 2 lamb chops).

Per Serving: Calories **241**   Fat **10.7g** (sat **3.6g**)   Protein **31.5g**   Carbohydrate **3.6g**   Fiber **0.4g**
Cholesterol **99mg**   Iron **2.7mg**   Sodium **89mg**   Calcium **43mg**
Exchanges: 4 Lean Meat

Marmalade Pork Chops

prep: 4 minutes   cook: 11 minutes

If you're cutting back on the amount of sodium in your diet, look for salt-free lemon-herb seasoning. The flavor is similar to lemon pepper seasoning, but without the salt. Serve with green beans and a Waldorf salad.

4   (4-ounce) boneless loin pork chops, trimmed
2   teaspoons lemon pepper seasoning
Cooking spray
1   teaspoon olive oil
2   tablespoons cider vinegar
¼   cup low-sugar orange marmalade

Sprinkle chops on both sides with lemon pepper seasoning.
Coat a large nonstick skillet with cooking spray; add oil, and place over medium-high heat until hot. Add chops to pan, and cook 5 minutes on each side or until done. Remove from pan, and keep warm.
Add vinegar to pan; stir in marmalade. Return chops to pan, turning once to coat; cook 1 minute or until thoroughly heated. Serve immediately.
Yield: 4 servings.

Per Serving: Calories **221**   Fat **9.4g** (sat **3.0g**)   Protein **25.1g**   Carbohydrate **7.1g**   Fiber **0.0g**
Cholesterol **71mg**   Iron **1.0mg**   Sodium **245mg**   Calcium **6mg**
Exchanges: ½ Starch, 3 Lean Meat

Peppered Pork
with Corn Relish *(photo, page 16)*

prep: 5 minutes   cook: 12 minutes

When chopping green onions and pepper, chop extra; then store in the freezer in zip-top plastic bags.

Cooking spray
4   (4-ounce) boneless center-cut loin pork chops (about ½ inch
        thick)
2   tablespoons jalapeño pepper jelly, divided
1½   cups frozen whole-kernel corn, thawed
½   cup chopped red bell pepper (1 small)
⅓   cup chopped green onions (about 3)

Heat a large nonstick skillet coated with cooking spray over medium heat. Add pork; top evenly with 1 tablespoon jelly. Cook pork 3 minutes on each side. Remove pork from pan, and keep warm.
Add remaining 1 tablespoon jelly to pan; cook over low heat, stirring constantly, until melted. Add corn, red bell pepper, and green onions; cook over medium-high heat, stirring constantly, 2 minutes. Add pork, and cook 3 minutes or until pork is done.
Yield: 4 servings (serving size: 1 chop and ½ cup relish).

Per Serving: Calories **268** Fat **8.8g** (sat **2.9g**) Protein **27.1g** Carbohydrate **20.8g** Fiber **2.0g**
Cholesterol **71mg** Iron **1.5mg** Sodium **82mg** Calcium **13mg**
Exchanges: 1 Starch, 1 Vegetable, 3 Lean Meat

Cumin-Rubbed Pork Chops

prep: 5 minutes   cook: 10 minutes

Serve with a tossed green salad drizzled with fat-free ranch-style dressing and with warm Corn Sticks (recipe on page 66).

4   (4-ounce) boneless center-cut loin pork chops
2   teaspoons ground cumin
¼   teaspoon salt
Cooking spray
1   cup diced peeled mango or papaya
1   cup rinsed and drained canned black beans
⅓   cup thick and chunky salsa
¼   cup chopped fresh cilantro or parsley

Prepare grill.
Sprinkle both sides of pork with cumin and salt; coat pork with cooking spray. Place pork on rack coated with cooking spray; cover and grill 5 minutes on each side or until done.
While pork grills, combine mango, beans, and salsa in a small bowl; toss gently to coat. Serve with pork chops; sprinkle with cilantro.
Yield: 4 servings (serving size: 1 chop and about ½ cup bean mixture).

Per Serving: Calories **315** Fat **9.6g** (sat **3.1g**) Protein **32.2g** Carbohydrate **25.7g** Fiber **4.0g**
Cholesterol **80mg** Iron **3.1mg** Sodium **434mg** Calcium **48mg**
Exchanges: 1 Starch, ½ Fruit, 4 Lean Meat

Pork Medallions
with Mustard Sauce

prep: 5 minutes   cook: 14 minutes

Change the flavor of this recipe by substituting different flavors of mustard such as brown, sweet-hot, or honey mustard. Serve with polenta and steamed broccoli.

1   (1-pound) pork tenderloin, trimmed
Cooking spray
1   teaspoon vegetable oil
½   cup fat-free milk
2   tablespoons Dijon mustard
3   green onions, sliced

Cut pork into 1-inch-thick slices. Place slices between two sheets of heavy-duty plastic wrap, and flatten to ½-inch thickness, using a meat mallet or rolling pin.

Coat a large nonstick skillet with cooking spray; add oil, and heat pan over medium-high heat. Add half of pork medallions, and cook 3 minutes on each side or until browned. Remove pork from pan; set aside, and keep warm. Repeat procedure with remaining half of pork medallions.

Reduce heat to low; add milk to pan, stirring constantly, scraping pan to loosen browned bits. Stir in mustard and green onions. Return pork to pan; cover and cook 2 minutes, turning to coat with sauce.

Yield: 4 servings.

Per Serving: Calories 160   Fat **4.7g** (sat **1.2g**)   Protein **24.9g**   Carbohydrate **2.4g**   Fiber **0.2g**
Cholesterol **74mg**   Iron **1.6mg**   Sodium **295mg**   Calcium **50mg**
Exchanges: 3½ Very Lean Meat

Sweet-Hot Pork Medallions

prep: 5 minutes   cook: 13 minutes

Sesame oil adds a rich, nutty flavor to this recipe, but you can use vegetable oil instead. Serve with roasted yellow squash and red bell peppers, and French bread.

1   (1-pound) pork tenderloin, trimmed
⅛   teaspoon dried crushed red pepper
⅛   teaspoon garlic powder
Cooking spray
1   teaspoon sesame oil
2   tablespoons water
2   tablespoons low-sodium soy sauce
2   tablespoons brown sugar

Cut pork into 1-inch-thick slices. Place slices between two sheets of heavy-duty plastic wrap, and flatten to ½-inch thickness, using a meat mallet or rolling pin. Sprinkle with pepper and garlic powder.
Coat a large nonstick skillet with cooking spray; add oil. Heat pan over medium-high heat. Add half of pork medallions, and cook 3 minutes on each side or until browned. Remove pork from pan; set aside, and keep warm. Repeat procedure with remaining half of pork medallions.
Add water, soy sauce, and brown sugar to pan. Reduce heat to medium; cook, stirring constantly, 1 minute or until bubbly. Spoon sauce evenly over pork.
Yield: 4 servings.

Per Serving: Calories 160   Fat **4.1g** (sat **1.1g**)   Protein **24.2g**   Carbohydrate **5.1g**   Fiber **0.0g**
Cholesterol **74mg**   Iron **1.7mg**   Sodium **299mg**   Calcium **13mg**
Exchanges: 3½ Very Lean Meat

Maple-Glazed Ham

prep: 5 minutes   cook: 7 minutes

If you're watching your sodium intake, you can use 33%-less-sodium ham. However, be aware that calories and fat are higher in the lower-sodium ham. Serve with mashed sweet potatoes and garden peas.

1   (8-ounce) slice lean cooked ham (about ¼ inch thick)
⅛   teaspoon freshly ground black pepper
Cooking spray
2   tablespoons maple syrup
1   teaspoon Dijon mustard
2   teaspoons cider vinegar

Cut ham slice into 3 pieces; sprinkle with pepper.
Heat a large nonstick skillet coated with cooking spray over medium-high heat. Add ham to pan, and cook 3 minutes on each side. Transfer ham to a serving platter, and keep warm.
Combine maple syrup, mustard, and vinegar in pan; stir well. Cook over medium heat, stirring constantly, 1 minute or until mixture is smooth and bubbly. Spoon glaze evenly over ham.
Yield: 3 servings.

Per Serving: Calories **129**   Fat **4.1g** (sat **0.0g**)   Protein **14.4g**   Carbohydrate **9.2g**   Fiber **0.0g**
Cholesterol **46mg**   Iron **0.7mg**   Sodium **1,111mg**   Calcium **14mg**
Exchanges: ½ Starch, 2 Lean Meat

Ham Steak with Pineapple Salsa

prep: 6 minutes   cook: 8 minutes

Serve with Roasted Sweet Potatoes and Onions (recipe on page 235) and steamed broccoli.

1   (15¼-ounce) can pineapple tidbits in juice, undrained
⅓   cup chopped green onions (3 small)
2   tablespoons brown sugar
1   tablespoon cider vinegar
2   teaspoons low-sodium soy sauce
2   garlic cloves, minced
¾   pound reduced-fat, lower-salt ham steak
Cooking spray

Prepare grill.
Drain pineapple, reserving juice. Combine pineapple, 2 tablespoons pineapple juice, green onions, and next 4 ingredients in a bowl; stir mixture well.
Place ham on grill rack covered with cooking spray; grill about 4 minutes on each side, basting often with remaining pineapple juice. Serve ham steak with pineapple salsa.
Yield: 4 servings (serving size: 3 ounces ham and about ½ cup salsa).

Per Serving: Calories **165**   Fat **3.4g** (sat **0.0g**)   Protein **12.1g**   Carbohydrate **23.3g**   Fiber **0.5g**
Cholesterol **31mg**   Iron **0.7mg**   Sodium **563mg**   Calcium **29mg**
Exchanges: 1½ Fruit, 2 Very Lean Meat

poultry

Creamed Chicken over Biscuits

prep: 5 minutes   cook: 10 minutes

Serve with sliced tomatoes and Citrusy Melon and Strawberry Cup (recipe on page 81).

1   (6-ounce) can flaky buttermilk biscuits (such as Hungry Jack)
Cooking spray
1   (9-ounce) package frozen diced cooked chicken breast
1   teaspoon minced garlic
1   (10-ounce) package frozen mixed vegetables, thawed and drained
1   (10¾-ounce) can condensed cream of roasted chicken with savory
        herbs soup, undiluted (such as Campbell's Healthy Request)
¼   cup dry white wine
¼   cup water
¼   teaspoon pepper

Bake biscuits according to package directions; set aside, and keep warm.

While biscuits bake, coat a large nonstick skillet with cooking spray; place over medium-high heat until hot. Add chicken and garlic; cook 5 minutes, stirring occasionally. Stir in vegetables and remaining 4 ingredients; cook over medium heat 5 minutes or until vegetables are tender and thoroughly heated, stirring often.

Split each biscuit in half, and place on each of 5 serving plates; spoon chicken mixture evenly over biscuits.

Yield: 5 servings.

Per Serving: Calories **254**   Fat **8.0g** (sat **2.2g**)   Protein **17.6g**   Carbohydrate **28.1g**   Fiber **2.2g**
Cholesterol **38mg**   Iron **1.5mg**   Sodium **718mg**   Calcium **0mg**
Exchanges: 1½ Starch, 1 Vegetable, 2 Very Lean Meat, 1 Fat

Skillet Chicken Divan

prep: 5 minutes   cook: 16 minutes

Round out the meal with a simple fruit salad.

1   family-sized bag quick-cooking boil-in-bag rice
Cooking spray
1   (9-ounce) package frozen diced cooked chicken breast
½   (16-ounce) package fresh broccoli florets
2   tablespoons water
1   (10¾-ounce) can condensed reduced-fat, reduced-sodium cream
      of chicken and broccoli soup, undiluted (such as Campbell's
      Healthy Request)
1   cup fat-free milk
½   cup (2 ounces) preshredded reduced-fat sharp Cheddar cheese
½   teaspoon curry powder
¼   teaspoon salt
¼   teaspoon pepper

Cook rice according to package directions, omitting salt and fat.
While rice cooks, heat a large nonstick skillet coated with cooking
spray over medium-high heat. Add chicken and broccoli; cook
6 minutes or until chicken is thawed and broccoli is crisp-tender,
adding 2 tablespoons water, if necessary, to prevent sticking.
Combine soup and remaining 5 ingredients, stirring well. Add to
broccoli mixture. Cook, uncovered, over medium-low heat 10 minutes,
stirring occasionally. Place ¾ cup cooked rice on each of 4 plates.
Spoon chicken mixture evenly over rice.
Yield: 4 servings.

Per Serving: Calories **409**   Fat **7.6g** (sat **3.0g**)   Protein **29.1g**   Carbohydrate **54.1g**   Fiber **2.2g**
Cholesterol **55mg**   Iron **2.5mg**   Sodium **703mg**   Calcium **266mg**
Exchanges: 2½ Starch, 2 Vegetable, 3 Lean Meat

Savory Chicken and Mushrooms

prep: 5 minutes   cook: 10 minutes

Serve with Sugared Carrots (recipe on page 229) and a fresh spinach salad.

Cooking spray
2   (8-ounce) packages presliced mushrooms
2   cups frozen diced cooked chicken breast
1   (10-ounce) container refrigerated light Alfredo sauce
       (such as Contadina)
¾   teaspoon dried thyme
¼   teaspoon salt
¼   teaspoon pepper
2   tablespoons dry sherry
4   slices whole wheat bread, toasted

Heat a large nonstick skillet coated with cooking spray over medium-high heat. Add mushrooms, and cook 5 minutes or until tender. Add chicken and next 4 ingredients; cook until thoroughly heated, stirring occasionally. Add sherry, stirring well.

Cut toast slices in half diagonally, and place on each of 4 serving plates. Spoon chicken mixture evenly over toast.

Yield: 4 servings.

Per Serving: Calories **276**   Fat **9.9g** (sat **4.4g**)   Protein **25.0g**   Carbohydrate **23.1g**   Fiber **2.6g**
Cholesterol **64mg**   Iron **3.0mg**   Sodium **768mg**   Calcium **149mg**
Exchanges: 1 Starch, 1 Vegetable, 3 Lean Meat

Spinach Pesto Couscous

prep: 7 minutes   cook: 7 minutes

Cheese-Stuffed Tomatoes (recipe on page 237) and warm focaccia compliment this nutritious dish.

1   teaspoon olive oil
¼   cup chopped walnuts
2   cups frozen diced cooked chicken breast, thawed
1⅓   cups water
1   (10-ounce) package frozen chopped spinach, thawed and
          well drained
1   (5.8-ounce) package roasted garlic and olive oil couscous
¼   cup thinly sliced fresh basil

Heat oil in a saucepan over medium-high heat; add walnuts, and cook 2 minutes or until toasted, stirring often. Remove walnuts from pan, and set aside.

Add chicken, water, spinach, contents of seasoning packet from couscous package, and basil to saucepan; cover, reduce heat, and simmer 2 minutes. Remove from heat, and stir in couscous. Cover and let stand 5 minutes. Stir in walnuts.

Yield: 4 servings (serving size: 1½ cups).

Per Serving: Calories **301**   Fat **8.8g** (sat **1.1g**)   Protein **23.1g**   Carbohydrate **34.5g**   Fiber **4.1g**
Cholesterol **37mg**   Iron **2.1mg**   Sodium **513mg**   Calcium **86mg**
Exchanges: 2 Starch, 1 Vegetable, 2 Lean Meat

Southwestern Chicken Hash

prep: 5 minutes   cook: 15 minutes

Tyson's frozen chopped cooked chicken is a great time-saver for this recipe, although it's more expensive than cooking it yourself. Serve with Corn Bread (recipe on page 63).

Cooking spray
1   (32-ounce) package frozen Southern-style hash brown potatoes
½   cup frozen chopped onion
2⅓ cups chopped cooked chicken breast
1   (14.5-ounce) can Mexican-style stewed tomatoes with jalapeño peppers and spices, undrained
1   (8¾-ounce) can whole-kernel corn, drained
½   teaspoon ground cumin
¼   teaspoon salt

Heat a large nonstick skillet coated with cooking spray over medium-high heat. Add potatoes and onion; cook 10 minutes or until browned, stirring often.

Add chicken and remaining ingredients to pan; cook 5 minutes or until thoroughly heated, stirring often.

Yield: 4 servings (serving size: about 3 cups).

Per Serving: Calories **338**   Fat **3.5g** (sat **0.9g**)   Protein **30.7g**   Carbohydrate **46.8g**   Fiber **3.2g**
Cholesterol **72mg**   Iron **2.2mg**   Sodium **721mg**   Calcium **38mg**
Exchanges: 3 Starch, 3 Very Lean Meat

Chicken à la King

prep: 5 minutes   cook: 10 minutes

Keep chopped, cooked chicken breast in the freezer so that you can easily assemble quick entrées like this one. For tender chunks of chicken every time, place 4 (4-ounce) skinless, boneless chicken breast halves on a baking sheet coated with cooking spray. Sprinkle the chicken with ¼ teaspoon each salt and pepper. Bake at 350° for 25 minutes. Cool slightly and chop. You'll have 4 servings, or about 3 cups, chopped, cooked chicken.

1   cup chopped cooked chicken breast
¼   cup fat-free milk
¼   cup frozen green peas, thawed
¼   teaspoon pepper
1   (10¾-ounce) can reduced-fat, reduced-sodium cream of chicken
        soup, undiluted (such as Campbell's Healthy Request)
1   (6-ounce) jar sliced mushrooms, drained
1   (2-ounce) jar diced pimiento, drained
2   tablespoons low-fat sour cream
2   slices reduced-calorie whole wheat bread, toasted
Paprika

Combine first 7 ingredients in a large saucepan; cook over low heat 10 minutes, stirring often. Remove from heat. Stir in sour cream.
Cut each slice of toast in half diagonally, if desired, and place on serving plates. Spoon chicken mixture over each serving of toast. Sprinkle with paprika.
Yield: 2 servings (serving size: 1 slice toast and 1¼ cups chicken mixture).

Per Serving: Calories **309** Fat **6.7g** (sat **2.6g**) Protein **32.2g** Carbohydrate **32.2g** Fiber **4.0g**
Cholesterol **88mg** Iron **3.1mg** Sodium **920mg** Calcium **126mg**
Exchanges: 2 Starch, 3½ Very Lean Meat, ½ Fat

Chicken Quesadillas

prep: 5 minutes   cook: 6 minutes

To seed tomatoes easily, cut them in half horizontally, and squeeze each half in your palm to remove the seeds.

1   cup frozen whole-kernel corn, thawed
½   cup chopped green pepper (about ½ large)
½   cup chopped seeded tomato (about 1 small)
2   tablespoons minced fresh cilantro
2   teaspoons balsamic vinegar
¼   teaspoon salt
1   cup chopped cooked chicken breast (about 5.5 ounces)
½   cup thick and chunky salsa
6   (6-inch) flour tortillas
¼   cup plus 2 tablespoons (1½ ounces) preshredded reduced-fat
        sharp Cheddar cheese
Cooking spray
Shredded lettuce (optional)

Combine first 6 ingredients; stir well, and set aside.
Combine chicken and salsa in a small bowl; arrange mixture evenly over 3 tortillas. Sprinkle evenly with cheese, and top with remaining tortillas.
Heat a medium nonstick skillet coated with cooking spray over medium-high heat. Place one quesadilla in pan. Cook 1 minute on each side or until golden. Repeat procedure with remaining quesadillas. Cut each quesadilla into 4 wedges. Arrange shredded lettuce on each of 4 serving plates, if desired. Place 3 quesadilla wedges over lettuce on each plate. Serve with corn salsa.
Yield: 4 servings (serving size: 3 quesadilla wedges and ½ cup corn salsa).

Per Serving: Calories **241** Fat **6.1g** (sat **2.0g**) Protein **20.5g** Carbohydrate **26.9g** Fiber **3.0g**
Cholesterol **43mg** Iron **2.1mg** Sodium **476mg** Calcium **154mg**
Exchanges: 2 Starch, 2 Lean Meat

Soft Chicken Tacos *(photo, cover)*

prep: 15 minutes   cook: 2 minutes

Everyone loves tacos. If you're making this for children, choose a milder salsa. Serve with a tomato-and-onion salad.

2	cups shredded roasted skinless, boneless chicken breast (about 11 ounces)
½	cup chopped fresh cilantro
½	cup bottled chipotle salsa (such as Frontera)
8	(6-inch) flour tortillas
1	cup chopped tomato (about 1 medium)
½	cup (2 ounces) preshredded reduced-fat Cheddar cheese
½	cup diced peeled avocado
¼	cup fat-free sour cream

Combine first 3 ingredients in a medium bowl, tossing well to combine. Spoon about ⅓ cup chicken mixture onto each tortilla; microwave each taco at HIGH 30 seconds or until warm.

Top each taco with 2 tablespoons tomato, 1 tablespoon cheese, 1 tablespoon avocado, and 1½ teaspoons sour cream; fold in half.

Yield: 4 servings (serving size: 2 tacos).

Per Serving: Calories **404** Fat **12.4g** (sat **4.0g**) Protein **33.0g** Carbohydrate **40.2g** Fiber **3.5g** Cholesterol **69mg** Iron **3.4mg** Sodium **623mg** Calcium **193mg**
Exchanges: 2½ Starch, 1 Vegetable, 3 Lean Meat

Barbecue Chicken Pizza

prep: 5 minutes   cook: 13 minutes

It's easier and even more flavorful to use roasted chicken available in the supermarket, but the sodium is much higher. Choose from the chicken cooked in the deli or the prepackaged roasted type. Just remember to remove the skin to keep the chicken low-fat. Serve with coleslaw and red grapes.

Cooking spray
1   (10-ounce) can refrigerated pizza crust dough
¾   cup chopped green bell pepper (about 1)
¾   cup thinly sliced red onion wedges (about 1 small onion)
½   cup honey barbecue sauce
1½ cups shredded cooked chicken breast (about 8.25 ounces)
1   cup (4 ounces) preshredded part-skim mozzarella cheese

Preheat oven to 425°.

Coat a 12-inch pizza pan or large baking sheet with cooking spray. Unroll dough, and press into pan. Bake at 425° for 5 minutes or until crust begins to brown.

While crust bakes, heat a medium nonstick skillet coated with cooking spray over medium-high heat. Add green bell pepper and onion, and sauté 5 minutes or until vegetables are tender.

Spread barbecue sauce evenly over baked crust; top evenly with chicken. Arrange vegetable mixture evenly over chicken; sprinkle with cheese. Bake at 425° for 8 minutes or until crust is golden and cheese melts.

Yield: 6 servings (serving size: 1 slice).

Per Serving: Calories **238**   Fat **5.5g** (sat **2.2g**)   Protein **16.2g**   Carbohydrate **21.3g**   Fiber **0.9g**
Cholesterol **35mg**   Iron **0.6mg**   Sodium **889mg**   Calcium **131mg**
Exchanges: 1 Starch, 1 Vegetable, 2 Lean Meat

Dijon Chicken Fettuccine

prep: 5 minutes   cook: 5 minutes

Serve with a romaine lettuce salad and a Strawberry Smoothie (recipe on page 42).

1   (9-ounce) package refrigerated fettuccine
½   (16-ounce) package fresh broccoli florets (4 cups)
⅓   cup fat-free honey Dijon dressing
¼   cup red wine vinegar
1   tablespoon Dijon mustard
1   teaspoon olive oil
1   teaspoon bottled minced garlic
1   (10-ounce) package cooked chicken breast (such as Tyson's roasted chicken), skinned and shredded
¼   teaspoon freshly ground black pepper

Cut pasta in half before cooking. Cook pasta according to package directions, omitting salt and fat. Add broccoli to pasta during the last 3 minutes of cooking time. Drain well; place in a large bowl.
While pasta cooks, combine dressing and next 4 ingredients; stir well. Pour dressing mixture over pasta mixture. Add chicken, and toss gently. Sprinkle with pepper.
Yield: 8 servings (serving size: 1 cup).

Per Serving: Calories **162**   Fat **2.4g** (sat **0.6g**)   Protein **12.5g**   Carbohydrate **22.9g**   Fiber **1.1g**
Cholesterol **54mg**   Iron **0.6mg**   Sodium **296mg**   Calcium **25mg**
Exchanges: 1 Starch, 1 Vegetable, 2 Very Lean Meat

Salsa Chicken on Polenta

prep: 5 minutes   cook: 15 minutes

Add some spice to traditional baked chicken with Mexican pepper-flavored polenta.

1   (16-ounce) tube refrigerated Mexican pepper-flavored polenta
Cooking spray
½   cup fat-free, less-sodium chicken broth
¾   cup chunky salsa
1   (15-ounce) can no-salt-added black beans, rinsed and drained
1   (8¾-ounce) can no-salt-added whole-kernel corn, drained
1   (9-ounce) package frozen cooked chicken breast strips, thawed
½   teaspoon ground cumin
2   tablespoons chopped fresh cilantro (optional)

Preheat oven to 500°.

Cut polenta crosswise into 8 slices; place on a baking sheet coated with cooking spray. Bake at 500° for 15 minutes or until thoroughly heated and golden around edges. Transfer polenta to each of 4 serving plates, and keep warm.

While polenta bakes, combine broth and next 5 ingredients in a large skillet; cover and bring to a boil. Reduce heat to medium-low; simmer, uncovered, 10 minutes, stirring occasionally. Stir in cilantro, if desired. Spoon chicken mixture over polenta, and serve immediately.

Yield: 4 servings (serving size: 2 polenta slices and about 1¼ cups chicken mixture).

Per Serving: Calories **291**   Fat **1.4g** (sat **0.8g**)   Protein **25.3g**   Carbohydrate **43.1g**   Fiber **8.9g**
Cholesterol **34mg**   Iron **3.2mg**   Sodium **593mg**   Calcium **76mg**
Exchanges: 2 Starch, 1 Vegetable, 3 Very Lean Meat

Lemon-Pepper Chicken

prep: 3 minutes   cook: 9 minutes

Use lemon pepper seasoning or any other lemon-herb seasoning in this recipe. If sodium is a concern, check the ingredient list on the seasoning label. The closer salt is to the beginning of the list, the higher the sodium content. Serve with couscous and snow peas.

Cooking spray
1   teaspoon olive oil
4   (4-ounce) skinless, boneless chicken breast halves
1¼ teaspoons lemon pepper seasoning
¼   cup fat-free, less-sodium chicken broth
¼   cup balsamic vinegar

Coat a large nonstick skillet with cooking spray; add oil, and place over medium-high heat until hot. While pan heats, sprinkle both sides of chicken breasts evenly with lemon pepper seasoning. Add chicken to pan, and cook 4 to 5 minutes on each side or until chicken is done. Transfer chicken to a serving platter, and keep warm.
Add broth and vinegar to pan; cook, stirring constantly, 1 minute or until slightly thickened. Spoon sauce over chicken.
Yield: 4 servings.

Per Serving: Calories **138**   Fat **2.7g** (sat **0.5g**)   Protein **26.2g**   Carbohydrate **0.3g**   Fiber **0.0g**
Cholesterol **66mg**   Iron **0.9mg**   Sodium **233mg**   Calcium **13mg**
Exchanges: 4 Very Lean Meat

Chicken Cacciatore

prep: 3 minutes   cook: 10 minutes

Quick-cooking boil-in-bag rice cooks in just 10 minutes. Serve with a tossed green salad and crusty French bread.

1   regular-sized bag quick-cooking boil-in-bag rice, uncooked, or
        2 cups hot cooked rice
Cooking spray
1   teaspoon olive oil
1   pound skinless, boneless chicken breast halves, cut into 1-inch
        pieces
1   cup frozen chopped green bell pepper
1   (14-ounce) jar chunky tomato, garlic, and onion pasta sauce
½   cup water
¼   teaspoon salt

Cook rice according to package directions, omitting salt and fat.
While rice cooks, coat a large nonstick skillet with cooking spray; add oil, and place over medium-high heat until hot. Add chicken and green pepper; sauté 5 minutes or until chicken is lightly browned.
Add pasta sauce, water, and salt to chicken mixture; bring to a boil. Cover, reduce heat, and simmer 5 minutes.
Add rice to chicken mixture, stirring well.
Yield: 4 servings (serving size: about 2 cups).

Per Serving: Calories 340   Fat **5.5g** (sat **0.9g**)   Protein **28.9g**   Carbohydrate **39.6g**   Fiber **3.1g**
Cholesterol **66mg**   Iron **2.0mg**   Sodium **634mg**   Calcium **24mg**
Exchanges: 2 Starch, 2 Vegetable, 3 Very Lean Meat

Cranberry-Apricot Chicken

prep: 7 minutes   cook: 13 minutes

Use kitchen scissors to slice the green onions and to chop the apricots. Coat the scissors with cooking spray before chopping the apricots, and the scissors won't get sticky. Serve with brown rice and a tossed green salad.

4   (4-ounce) skinless, boneless chicken breast halves
½   teaspoon ground sage
Olive oil-flavored cooking spray
1   teaspoon olive oil
⅔   cup fat-free, less-sodium chicken broth, divided
1   teaspoon cornstarch
⅓   cup sweetened dried cranberries
⅓   cup chopped dried apricot halves
⅓   cup sliced green onions (about 3)

Place each chicken breast half between two sheets of heavy-duty plastic wrap; flatten to ¼-inch thickness, using a meat mallet or rolling pin. Sprinkle sage evenly over chicken.

Coat a large nonstick skillet with cooking spray; add oil, and place over medium-high heat until hot. Add chicken, and cook 3 minutes on each side or until chicken is lightly browned.

Combine 1 tablespoon broth and cornstarch; stir well, and set aside. Add cranberries, apricot, and remaining broth to pan. Bring mixture to a boil; cover, reduce heat, and simmer 6 minutes or until chicken and fruit are tender. Transfer chicken to a serving platter.

Stir cornstarch mixture; add to pan. Stir in green onions, and cook, stirring constantly, 1 minute or until sauce thickens. Serve sauce over chicken.

Yield: 4 servings (serving size: 1 chicken breast half and about ⅓ cup sauce).

Per Serving: Calories **213**   Fat **2.7g** (sat **0.5g**)   Protein **26.5g**   Carbohydrate **18.3g**   Fiber **1.7g**
Cholesterol **66mg**   Iron **0.9mg**   Sodium **155mg**   Calcium **18mg**
Exchanges: 1 Fruit, 4 Very Lean Meat

Hawaiian Chicken with Pineapple Salsa

prep: 5 minutes   cook: 12 minutes

We suggest serving this taste-of-the-islands chicken with steamed white rice and Sugar Snap Peas with Cashews (recipe on page 232).

4   (4-ounce) skinless, boneless chicken breast halves
1   teaspoon ground coriander
½   teaspoon salt
Cooking spray
¼   cup pineapple preserves, divided
1   (15¼-ounce) can pineapple tidbits in juice, drained
¼   cup chopped fresh cilantro
1   tablespoon seasoned rice vinegar
2   teaspoons minced jalapeño pepper

Place each chicken breast half between two sheets of heavy-duty plastic wrap; pound to ¼-inch thickness, using a meat mallet or rolling pin. Sprinkle chicken with coriander and salt; coat with cooking spray.
Heat a large nonstick skillet coated with cooking spray over medium heat. Add chicken, and cook 5 to 6 minutes on each side or until chicken is done. Add 2 tablespoons preserves to pan; cook until chicken is glazed, turning once.
Combine remaining 2 tablespoons preserves, pineapple, and remaining 3 ingredients in a bowl; stir well. Serve with chicken.
Yield: 4 servings.

Per Serving: Calories **232** Fat **1.7g** (sat **0.4g**) Protein **26.8g** Carbohydrate **27.7g** Fiber **0.6g**
Cholesterol **66mg** Iron **1.5mg** Sodium **377mg** Calcium **36mg**
Exchanges: 2 Fruit, 3 Very Lean Meat

Peachy Chicken and Rice

prep: 5 minutes   cook: 15 minutes

*This recipe is even more attractive if you use 1 small red bell pepper
and 1 small green bell pepper. Red peppers are usually more expensive,
but they have a sweeter, more mellow flavor than the green ones. Serve
with soft dinner rolls.*

1   regular-sized bag quick-cooking boil-in-bag rice, uncooked,
        or 2 cups hot cooked rice
Cooking spray
1   pound skinless, boneless chicken breast halves, cut into
        1-inch pieces
½   cup chopped onion (about 1 small)
1   cup chopped green bell pepper (about 1 large)
1   (8-ounce) can sliced water chestnuts, drained
⅓   cup barbecue sauce
⅓   cup low-sugar peach preserves
2   tablespoons low-sodium soy sauce

Cook rice according to package directions, omitting salt and fat.
While rice cooks, heat a large nonstick skillet coated with cooking
spray over medium-high heat. Add chicken, onion, and pepper; cook
5 minutes or until chicken is lightly browned and vegetables are crisp-
tender. Add water chestnuts and remaining 3 ingredients to pan. Cover,
reduce heat, and simmer 10 minutes.
Arrange rice on a serving platter. Spoon chicken mixture over rice.
Yield: 4 servings.

Per Serving: Calories **337** Fat **2.3g** (sat **0.5g**) Protein **29.8g** Carbohydrate **46.3g** Fiber **1.8g**
Cholesterol **66mg** Iron **2.7mg** Sodium **496mg** Calcium **37mg**
Exchanges: 3 Starch, 3 Very Lean Meat

Turkey Patties with Piquant Sauce

prep: 5 minutes   cook: 9 minutes

The thicker the patties, the longer it will take them to cook. Serve with steamed green beans and baby carrots.

1   pound ground turkey
½   cup chopped red onion (about 1 small)
1   tablespoon dried parsley flakes
2   tablespoons plain fat-free yogurt
Cooking spray
2   tablespoons brown sugar
2   tablespoons reduced-calorie ketchup
1   teaspoon dry mustard

Preheat broiler.

Combine first 4 ingredients in a large bowl, mixing well. Shape mixture into 4 patties.

Place patties on broiler pan coated with cooking spray; broil 4 or 5 minutes on each side or until done.

While patties broil, combine sugar, ketchup, and dry mustard, stirring well. Spread mixture evenly over tops of patties; broil 30 seconds or just until ketchup mixture begins to bubble.

Yield: 4 servings (serving size: 1 patty).

Per Serving: Calories **177**   Fat **4.5g** (sat **1.4g**)   Protein **25.4g**   Carbohydrate **7.0g**   Fiber **0.3g**
Cholesterol **64mg**   Iron **1.8mg**   Sodium **69mg**   Calcium **43mg**
Exchanges: ½ Starch, 3½ Very Lean Meat

Southwestern-Style Spaghetti

prep: 5 minutes   cook: 15 minutes

Serve with a romaine and endive salad drizzled with fat-free ranch dressing, and pass around a basket of chewy breadsticks.

4   ounces uncooked spaghetti
8   ounces ground turkey breast
½   cup frozen chopped onion
1½   teaspoons bottled minced garlic
1   teaspoon ground cumin
1   (14½-ounce) can salsa-style tomatoes, undrained
½   cup picante sauce
¼   cup chopped fresh cilantro
2   tablespoons preshredded part-skim mozzarella cheese

Cook spaghetti according to package directions, omitting salt and fat. Drain well, and place on a small serving platter.
While spaghetti cooks, cook turkey and next 3 ingredients in a large saucepan over medium heat until browned, stirring until turkey crumbles. Add tomatoes and picante sauce to turkey mixture; simmer, uncovered, 10 minutes or until slightly thickened. Spoon over spaghetti; sprinkle with cilantro and cheese.
Yield: 3 servings.

Per Serving: Calories **305** Fat **2.7g** (sat **1.0g**) Protein **27.1g** Carbohydrate **43.6g** Fiber **4.0g**
Cholesterol **48mg** Iron **4.6mg** Sodium **917mg** Calcium **73mg**
Exchanges: 2 Starch, 2 Vegetable, 3 Very Lean Meat

Turkey Cutlets in Orange Sauce

prep: 5 minutes   cook: 8 minutes

The orange sauce in this recipe is delicious with chicken or pork, too.
Instead of turkey cutlets, substitute pounded boneless chicken breast
halves or pork tenderloin slices. Serve with orzo and steamed snow peas.

2	teaspoons vegetable oil
1	pound turkey breast cutlets
2	tablespoons all-purpose flour
⅓	cup sliced green onions (about 2 medium)
⅛	teaspoon garlic powder
¾	cup orange juice
1	tablespoon low-sodium soy sauce

Orange slices (optional)

Add oil to a large nonstick skillet, and place over medium-high heat
until hot. While pan heats, dredge turkey cutlets in flour. Add turkey to
hot pan, and cook 3 minutes or until browned, turning once. Remove
turkey from pan.

Reduce heat to medium-high; add green onions and garlic powder;
sauté 30 seconds. Add orange juice and soy sauce to pan; bring to a
boil. Cook, stirring constantly, 2 minutes or until mixture thickens
slightly.

Return turkey to pan; simmer 2 minutes or until turkey is thoroughly
heated. Transfer to a serving platter. Garnish with orange slices, if
desired.

Yield: 4 servings (serving size: 3 ounces turkey plus sauce).

Per Serving: Calories 190   Fat **4.1g** (sat **1.0g**)   Protein **27.7**   Carbohydrate **8.8g**   Fiber **0.3g**
Cholesterol **68mg**   Iron **1.7mg**   Sodium **194mg**   Calcium **23mg**
Exchanges: ½ Fruit, 4 Very Lean Meat

Balsamic Turkey

prep: 5 minutes   cook: 9 minutes

Serve with greek-style rice and Sugar Snap Peas with Cashews (recipe on page 232).

¾   pound turkey breast cutlets
¼   teaspoon salt
¼   teaspoon garlic powder
¼   teaspoon pepper
Cooking spray
1   teaspoon olive oil
1   large red bell pepper, sliced into rings
¼   cup balsamic vinegar

Rub turkey with salt, garlic powder, and ¼ teaspoon pepper. Coat a large nonstick skillet with cooking spray. Add oil, and place pan over medium-high heat until hot. Add turkey, and cook 2 minutes on each side or until lightly browned. Transfer cutlets to a serving platter; keep warm.

Add red bell pepper to pan, and sauté 3 minutes or until crisp-tender. Transfer red pepper to serving platter. Add vinegar to pan; cook 2 minutes or until slightly reduced. Spoon over cutlets.

Yield: 3 servings (serving size: 3 ounces turkey, about ⅓ cup pepper, and 3 tablespoons vinegar).

Per Serving: Calories **157**   Fat **3.6g** (sat **1.0g**)   Protein **27.1g**   Carbohydrate **2.5g**   Fiber **0.7g**
Cholesterol **68mg**   Iron **2.0mg**   Sodium **268mg**   Calcium **17mg**
Exchanges: 3 Lean Meat

Lemon Turkey and Asparagus

prep: 5 minutes   cook: 7 minutes

Thaw the asparagus in the microwave while you combine the chicken broth mixture, chop the pepper, and cut the turkey. Serve with rice and dinner rolls.

½   cup fat-free, less-sodium chicken broth
2   tablespoons lemon juice
1   tablespoon low-sodium soy sauce
2   teaspoons cornstarch
¼   teaspoon freshly ground black pepper
Cooking spray
2   teaspoons vegetable oil, divided
1   (9-ounce) package frozen asparagus cuts, thawed
1   small red bell pepper, chopped
1   pound turkey tenderloin, cut into 1-inch pieces

Combine first 5 ingredients, stirring well; set aside. Heat a large nonstick skillet coated with cooking spray over medium-high heat; add 1 teaspoon oil. Add asparagus and red bell pepper; sauté 2 minutes or until tender. Transfer to a bowl; set aside, and keep warm.
Add remaining 1 teaspoon oil and turkey to pan. Cook 3 minutes or until turkey is browned, stirring occasionally. Stir broth mixture, and add to pan; cook 2 minutes or until mixture is thickened and bubbly. Return asparagus mixture to pan. Stir just until coated.
Yield: 4 servings.

Per Serving: Calories 190   Fat **4.2g** (sat **1.0g**)   Protein **28.8g**   Carbohydrate **7.4g**   Fiber **1.4g**
Cholesterol **68mg**   Iron **1.9mg**   Sodium **318mg**   Calcium **18mg**
Exchanges: 1 Vegetable, 4 Very Lean Meat

Turkey Sausage with Peppers

prep: 8 minutes   cook: 10 minutes

You can substitute other types of low-fat turkey sausage for Italian style. Italian turkey sausages often have a strong taste of fennel seeds, a spice with a licorice-like flavor.

8   ounces turkey Italian sausage (about 2 links)
Cooking spray
1   medium onion, sliced
1   medium green bell pepper, sliced
1   medium red bell pepper, sliced
⅓   cup dry white wine

Remove casings from sausage. Cut sausage into 1½-inch pieces.
Heat a large nonstick skillet coated with cooking spray over medium-high heat. Add sausage, onion, and peppers; cook 8 to 10 minutes or until sausage is browned and vegetables are tender, stirring occasionally.
Add wine to pan. Bring to a boil; reduce heat, and simmer 2 to 3 minutes or until sauce is slightly thickened, stirring occasionally.
Yield: 2 servings.

Per Serving: Calories **242**   Fat **11.2g** (sat **3.1g**)   Protein **21.2g**   Carbohydrate **15.0g**   Fiber **3.8g**
Cholesterol **90mg**   Iron **2.1mg**   Sodium **650mg**   Calcium **27mg**
Exchanges: 2 Vegetable, 2 Medium-Fat Meat

Penne with Beans and Sausage

prep: 5 minutes   cook: 10 minutes

For a nice change, try substituting sun-dried tomato-flavored penne for the plain.

8   ounces uncooked penne or sun-dried tomato-flavored penne (such as Mendocino)
6   ounces fat-free smoked turkey sausage (such as Butterball)
Cooking spray
½   cup fat-free, less-sodium chicken broth
1   cup cannellini beans or other white beans, rinsed and drained
2   cups loosely packed baby spinach leaves or torn spinach leaves
3   tablespoons red wine vinegar
1   large tomato, chopped

Cook pasta according to package directions, omitting salt and fat. Drain well, and return to saucepan.

While pasta cooks, cut sausage in half lengthwise; cut each half into thin slices. Coat a large nonstick skillet with cooking spray; add sausage, and cook 4 minutes, stirring occasionally. Add broth and beans; cook until thoroughly heated.

Add sausage mixture, spinach, vinegar, and tomato to pasta; toss well.

Yield: 6 servings (serving size: 1½ cups).

Per Serving: Calories **223**   Fat **1.6g** (sat **0.0g**)   Protein **13.8g**   Carbohydrate **38.1g**   Fiber **5.5g**
Cholesterol **13mg**   Iron **1.9mg**   Sodium **262mg**   Calcium **36mg**
Exchanges: 1½ Starch, 1 Vegetable, 2 Very Lean Meat

salads

Frozen Cherry Salad

prep: 8 minutes   freeze: 8 hours

You can serve this recipe as a creamy salad or a refreshing dessert.

1   (20-ounce) can light cherry pie filling
1   (14-ounce) can fat-free sweetened condensed milk
1   (8-ounce) can crushed pineapple in juice, drained
1   tablespoon lemon juice
1   (8-ounce) container frozen reduced-calorie whipped topping,
        thawed
Cooking spray

Combine first 4 ingredients; fold in whipped topping.
Coat an 8-inch square pan with cooking spray; pour cherry mixture
into prepared pan. Cover and freeze 8 hours or overnight. Cut into
10 equal rectangles. Serve immediately.
Yield: 10 servings (serving size: 1 rectangle).

Per Serving: Calories **217** Fat **3.0g** (sat **3.0g**) Protein **3.7g** Carbohydrate **43.4g** Fiber **0.9g**
Cholesterol **0mg** Iron **0.0mg** Sodium **65mg** Calcium **17mg**
Exchanges: 1 Starch, 2 Fruit, ½ Fat

Pineapple-Mango Salad

prep: 15 minutes   stand: 10 minutes

Both pineapple and mango are good sources of vitamin C, a powerful nutrient that protects the body from harmful free radicals.

¾ cup cubed peeled ripe mango (about 1 medium)
1 cup cubed fresh pineapple
¾ cup chopped red bell pepper (about 1 medium)
1 orange
2 tablespoons finely chopped jalapeño pepper (about 1)
1½ tablespoons sugar

Combine mango, pineapple, and red bell pepper in a medium bowl; set aside.
Grate 1 teaspoon rind from orange; set aside. Peel and section orange over a small bowl, reserving 2 tablespoons juice. Discard remaining juice and membranes. Add reserved orange rind and sections to mango mixture. Add jalapeño pepper, reserved orange juice, and sugar; toss gently. Let stand 10 minutes.
Yield: 5 servings (serving size: about ½ cup).

Per Serving: Calories **77** Fat **0.2g** (sat **0.1g**) Protein **0.6g** Carbohydrate **19.2g** Fiber **2.0g**
Cholesterol **0mg** Iron **0.5mg** Sodium **2mg** Calcium **17mg**
Exchanges: 1½ Fruit

• vegetarian •

Fig and Blue Cheese Salad

prep: 5 minutes

Instead of figs, you can substitute 2 sliced fresh peaches, Red Delicious apples, or 4 sliced fresh apricots. Serve the salad with beef tenderloin and roasted asparagus.

4   cups torn red leaf lettuce leaves
3   tablespoons rice vinegar
1   teaspoon extravirgin olive oil
8   fresh figs or dried figs, quartered
½   cup (2 ounces) crumbled blue cheese
Freshly ground black pepper

Place lettuce in a large bowl; set aside. Combine vinegar and oil in a small bowl, stirring well with a wire whisk. Pour dressing over lettuce; toss well.

Arrange salad mixture evenly on each of 4 salad plates. Arrange fig quarters evenly over salads; sprinkle evenly with cheese. Sprinkle evenly with pepper. Serve immediately.

Yield: 4 servings.

Per Serving: Calories **142**   Fat **5.6g** (sat **2.9g**)   Protein **4.3g**   Carbohydrate **21.4g**   Fiber **4.4g**
Cholesterol **11mg**   Iron **1.0mg**   Sodium **203mg**   Calcium **135mg**
Exchanges: 1 Fruit, 1 Vegetable, 1 Fat

Fruit and Honey Spinach Salad

prep: 13 minutes

To save time, look for sliced mango in a jar. It's usually in the produce section of the supermarket. Serve with grilled fish and steamed yellow squash.

⅓   cup white balsamic vinegar
2   tablespoons honey
½   (10-ounce) package fresh spinach (about 6 cups), torn
1   firm ripe mango, peeled and cut into thin slices
1   cup raspberries or blueberries

Combine vinegar and honey in a small bowl, stirring well with a wire whisk. Place spinach in a large bowl; pour ¼ cup vinegar mixture over spinach, and toss well.

Arrange spinach mixture evenly on each of 4 salad plates. Arrange mango slices and raspberries evenly over spinach; drizzle remaining vinegar mixture evenly over salads. Serve immediately.

Yield: 4 servings.

Per Serving: Calories **83**   Fat **0.4g** (sat **0.1g**)   Protein **1.6g**   Carbohydrate **20.6g**   Fiber **4.7g**
Cholesterol **0mg**   Iron **1.3mg**   Sodium **29mg**   Calcium **47mg**
Exchanges: 1 Fruit, 1 Vegetable

• vegetarian •

Lemony Strawberry-Spinach Salad

prep: 15 minutes

A light, lemony vinaigrette adds a refreshing twist to this traditional strawberry-spinach salad.

1   (10-ounce) package fresh spinach, torn
2   cups sliced strawberries
½   cup thinly sliced red onion (½ small)
⅓   cup fresh lemon juice (2 lemons)
3   tablespoons sugar
1   tablespoon vegetable oil
2   teaspoons grated lemon rind
Freshly ground black pepper

Combine first 3 ingredients in a large bowl.
Combine lemon juice, sugar, and oil in a small bowl; stir with a whisk until blended. Stir in lemon rind. Pour over spinach mixture; toss. Sprinkle with pepper. Serve immediately.

Yield: 6 servings (serving size: 2 cups).

Per Serving: Calories **75** Fat **2.6g** (sat **0.5g**) Protein **1.8g** Carbohydrate **12.9g** Fiber **3.1g**
Cholesterol **0mg** Iron **1.6mg** Sodium **38mg** Calcium **58mg**
Exchanges: 2 Vegetable, ½ Fat

Spring Greens with Strawberries and Honey-Watermelon Dressing

prep: 15 minutes

Store fresh strawberries in the refrigerator for two to three days. Wash them, and remove their green caps just before using.

1   cup cubed seeded watermelon
1½ tablespoons honey
1   tablespoon raspberry vinegar
1   tablespoon vegetable oil
¼   teaspoon salt
5   cups gourmet salad greens
1¼ cups sliced strawberries
½   cup thinly sliced red onion (½ small)
⅓   cup sliced almonds, toasted
Freshly ground black pepper

Combine first 5 ingredients in a blender; process until smooth, stopping once to scrape down sides.
Place 1 cup greens on each of 5 salad plates. Top evenly with strawberries, red onion, and almonds. Drizzle 2 tablespoons dressing over each salad. Sprinkle evenly with pepper. Serve immediately.
Yield: 5 servings.

Per Serving: Calories **113** Fat **6.1g** (sat **0.8g**) Protein **2.7g** Carbohydrate **13.9g** Fiber **2.9g**
Cholesterol **0mg** Iron **1.1mg** Sodium **124mg** Calcium **45mg**
Exchanges: 1 Vegetable, ½ Fruit, 1 Fat

• vegetarian •

Lemon-Dill-White Bean Salad

prep: 8 minutes

Beans are a terrific source of folate, the nutrient that helps prevent certain birth defects. It also lowers homocysteine levels (high levels are linked to heart disease and heart attack).

1   (16-ounce) can navy beans, rinsed and drained
½   cup chopped green onions (about 4)
2   tablespoons chopped fresh dill
1   tablespoon extravirgin olive oil
1   tablespoon lemon juice
½   teaspoon salt
8   slices tomato (about 1 large)
1   lemon, quartered (optional)

Combine first 6 ingredients in a medium bowl, tossing gently. Place 2 tomato slices on each of 4 salad plates; top each serving with ½ cup bean mixture. Serve with a lemon wedge, if desired.

Yield: 4 servings.

Per Serving: Calories **122** Fat **3.9g** (sat **0.6g**) Protein **5.7g** Carbohydrate **17.4g** Fiber **4.0g**
Cholesterol **0mg** Iron **1.7mg** Sodium **541mg** Calcium **43mg**
Exchanges: 1 Starch, ½ Vegetable, ½ Fat

Caesar Salad

prep: 6 minutes

To keep preparation time to a minimum, buy 2 (10-ounce) packages romaine salad, available in the produce section of your grocery store.

¼ cup water
3 tablespoons white wine vinegar
2 tablespoons olive oil
1 tablespoon Dijon mustard
1 teaspoon Worcestershire sauce
½ teaspoon garlic pepper (such as Lawry's)
2 garlic cloves, crushed
10 cups torn romaine lettuce
1 cup fat-free Caesar-flavored croutons
2 tablespoons freshly shredded Parmesan cheese
Freshly ground black pepper

Combine first 7 ingredients in a small bowl; stir well with a whisk.
Combine lettuce and dressing in a large bowl; toss well. Add croutons and cheese; toss well. Sprinkle with pepper. Serve immediately.
Yield: 10 servings (serving size: 1 cup).

Per Serving: Calories **49** Fat **3.2g** (sat **0.6g**) Protein **1.3g** Carbohydrate **3.2g** Fiber **0.7g**
Cholesterol **1mg** Iron **0.4mg** Sodium **119mg** Calcium **26mg**
Exchanges: 1 Vegetable, ½ Fat

Steak Caesar Salad for Two

prep: 5 minutes   cook: 4 minutes

Serve this main-dish salad with toasted French bread slices. Before toasting, lightly spray each slice with olive oil-flavored cooking spray, and sprinkle with garlic powder.

1   tablespoon no-salt-added lemon pepper seasoning
½   pound boneless sirloin steak (¾ inch thick), trimmed
Cooking spray
5   cups torn romaine lettuce
¼   cup fat-free seasoned croutons
¼   cup fat-free Caesar dressing
6   cherry tomatoes, halved

Preheat broiler.
Rub lemon pepper seasoning on both sides of steak; place steak on a broiler pan coated with cooking spray. Broil 2 to 3 minutes on each side or until steak is done.
While steak broils, combine lettuce and remaining 3 ingredients in a large bowl; toss gently. Arrange on each of 2 salad plates.
Slice steak into thin strips, and arrange evenly over lettuce.
Yield: 2 servings.

Per Serving: Calories **271**   Fat **7.1g** (sat **2.6g**)   Protein **30.0g**   Carbohydrate **20.2g**   Fiber **2.0g**
Cholesterol **80mg**   Iron **4.1mg**   Sodium **535mg**   Calcium **42mg**
Exchanges: ½ Starch, 2 Vegetable, 3 Lean Meat

Fruited Chef's Salad with Garlic Croutons

prep: 5 minutes   cook: 8 minutes

Angel food cake topped with fresh strawberries is the perfect dessert complement for this salad.

½ (8-ounce) loaf French bread, cut into 12 slices
Garlic-flavored cooking spray
2 tablespoons chopped walnuts
8 cups packed mixed baby salad greens
1 ripe pear, cored and diced (about 1¼ cups)
4 ounces reduced-sodium deli ham, cut into thin strips
¼ cup (1 ounce) crumbled blue cheese
⅓ cup fat-free raspberry vinaigrette

Preheat oven to 400°.
Spray both sides of bread slices with cooking spray. Arrange bread on a large baking sheet, and bake at 400° for 4 minutes. Turn bread; add walnuts to baking sheet, and bake 4 minutes or until croutons are golden.
While croutons bake, arrange salad greens evenly on each of 4 salad plates. Arrange pear, ham, and cheese evenly over greens. Drizzle vinaigrette evenly over salads, and sprinkle with toasted walnuts. Serve each salad with 3 toasted croutons.
Yield: 4 servings.

Per Serving: Calories **203**   Fat **6.4g** (sat **1.7g**)   Protein **11.1g**   Carbohydrate **26.8g**   Fiber **2.7g**
Cholesterol **20mg**   Iron **2.0mg**   Sodium **638mg**   Calcium **115mg**
Exchanges: 1 Starch, ½ Fruit, 1 Vegetable, 1 Lean Meat

Salad Niçoise *(photo, page 4)*

prep: 9 minutes   cook: 8 minutes

Niçoise is a French phrase meaning "as prepared in Nice." This salad is typical of what you might find while dining in that French city.

3   small red potatoes, sliced
¼   pound green beans
1   (8-ounce) tuna steak (about ¾ inch thick)
⅓   cup white wine vinegar
1½   tablespoons lemon juice
1½   teaspoons Dijon mustard
2   cups torn Bibb lettuce or leaf lettuce
1   tomato, cut into eight wedges
¼   teaspoon freshly ground black pepper

Arrange potato and green beans on one side of a vegetable steamer over boiling water in a Dutch oven. Place tuna on opposite side of steamer. Cover and steam 8 to 10 minutes or until fish flakes easily when tested with a fork. Set tuna aside to cool. Plunge potato and beans into ice water to cool.

While tuna and vegetables steam, combine vinegar, lemon juice, and mustard in a jar; cover tightly, and shake vigorously.

Place lettuce on a serving platter. Drain potato and beans; arrange over lettuce. Flake tuna, and place on salad; add tomato wedges. Drizzle evenly with vinegar mixture. Sprinkle with freshly ground pepper.

Yield: 2 servings.

Per Serving: Calories **279** Fat **6.2g** (sat **1.5g**) Protein **30.5g** Carbohydrate **26.5g** Fiber **3.8g**
Cholesterol **43mg** Iron **3.4mg** Sodium **173mg** Calcium **37mg**
Exchanges: 1½ Starch, 1 Vegetable, 4 Very Lean Meat

Beef Salad Olé

prep: 5 minutes

We made this recipe with leftover lean eye-of-round roast. You can substitute deli roast beef, but it will be higher in sodium. Serve with warm fat-free tortillas.

½   cup fat-free Italian dressing
½   teaspoon ground cumin
4   ounces shredded lean roast beef (about ⅔ cup)
1   (15-ounce) can no-salt-added kidney beans or no-salt-added
      black beans, rinsed and drained
¾   cup (3 ounces) shredded or cubed Monterey Jack cheese with
      jalapeño peppers
1   (11-ounce) can Mexican-style corn, drained
1½ cups finely chopped plum tomatoes (about 4)
4   green leaf lettuce leaves

Combine dressing and cumin in a large bowl, stirring well. Add beef and next 4 ingredients, tossing gently to combine. Serve immediately, or cover and chill up to 8 hours, if desired.

To serve, arrange lettuce on each of 4 serving plates. Spoon salad evenly over lettuce.

Yield: 4 servings.

Per Serving: Calories **260** Fat **5.7g** (sat **2.9g**) Protein **20.1g** Carbohydrate **33.6g** Fiber **3.6g**
Cholesterol **27mg** Iron **2.7mg** Sodium **891mg** Calcium **200mg**
Exchanges: 2 Starch, 1 Vegetable, 2 Lean Meat

Curried Chicken Salad

prep: 11 minutes

Serve this chicken salad with a fresh fruit bowl of cubed cantaloupe and red grapes.

¼ cup plain fat-free yogurt
¼ cup reduced-fat mayonnaise
¾ to 1 teaspoon curry powder
¼ teaspoon bottled minced ginger
⅛ teaspoon salt
1 rotisserie chicken, meat removed and chopped (about 2 cups)
1 cup packaged preshredded carrot
½ cup chopped green onions (about 4)
¼ cup raisins, coarsely chopped
Leaf lettuce leaves (optional)

Combine first 5 ingredients in a small bowl; stir well. Add chicken and next 3 ingredients; stir to coat. Serve over lettuce leaves, if desired.
Yield: 3 servings (serving size: 1 cup).

Per Serving: Calories **262** Fat **12.9g** (sat **2.7g**) Protein **22.8g** Carbohydrate **15.8g** Fiber **1.7g**
Cholesterol **98mg** Iron **2.0mg** Sodium **887mg** Calcium **61mg**
Exchanges: 1 Fruit, 3 Lean Meat, 1 Fat

Grilled Chicken and Raspberry Salad

prep: 5 minutes   cook: 10 minutes

Italian salad mix is a combination of romaine lettuce and radicchio.
A 10-ounce bag contains about 6 cups. Consider serving this salad
with Lemon-Blueberry Muffins (recipe on page 61).

¼   cup balsamic vinegar
3   tablespoons seedless raspberry jam
4   (4-ounce) skinless, boneless chicken breast halves
Cooking spray
1   (10-ounce) package ready-to-eat Italian salad mix
1   cup raspberries
Freshly ground black pepper

Prepare grill.
While grill heats, combine vinegar and jam in a small bowl, stirring
with a whisk until smooth. Reserve 3 tablespoons vinegar mixture.
Brush remaining ¼ cup vinegar mixture evenly over each chicken
breast. Place chicken on grill rack coated with cooking spray; cover
and grill 5 minutes on each side or until chicken is done. Set chicken
aside.
Place lettuce mix in a large bowl; pour reserved 3 tablespoons vinegar
mixture over lettuce, and toss well. Arrange lettuce mixture evenly on
each of 4 serving plates.
Cut chicken crosswise into thin strips; arrange chicken strips evenly on
lettuce mixture. Top evenly with raspberries. Sprinkle evenly with pepper.
Yield: 4 servings.

Per Serving: Calories **238**   Fat **3.9g** (sat **1.0g**)   Protein **32.0g**   Carbohydrate **16.7g**   Fiber **3.5g**
Cholesterol **84mg**   Iron **1.3mg**   Sodium **81mg**   Calcium **23mg**
Exchanges: 1 Vegetable, 1 Fruit, 4 Very Lean Meat

Garlicky Bean and Spinach Salad

prep: 12 minutes

Spinach offers a powerhouse of nutrients. It's loaded with folate, beta carotene, and vitamin C. Spinach also contains some of the highest levels of lutein of any vegetable. This phytochemical protects the eyes from harmful ultraviolet rays.

2¼ cups coarsely chopped spinach
1 (15-ounce) can navy beans, rinsed and drained
½ cup thinly sliced red onion (½ small)
1 tablespoon cider vinegar
1 tablespoon extravirgin olive oil
1 garlic clove, minced
¼ teaspoon salt
⅛ teaspoon pepper

Combine first 3 ingredients in a large bowl. Combine vinegar and remaining 4 ingredients in a small bowl; add to bean mixture, tossing gently to coat. Serve immediately.

Yield: 4 servings (serving size: 1 cup).

Per Serving: Calories **154** Fat **3.9g** (sat **0.6g**) Protein **8.4g** Carbohydrate **22.8g** Fiber **6.1g**
Cholesterol **0mg** Iron **2.8mg** Sodium **478mg** Calcium **82mg**
Exchanges: 1 Starch, 1 Vegetable, ½ Very Lean Meat, ½ Fat

Marinated Bean Salad

prep: 12 minutes   cook: 2 minutes   chill: 8 hours

Prepare the salad ahead of time, and pull it out of the refrigerator just before serving.

1   (15-ounce) can dark red kidney beans, rinsed and drained
1   (15¼-ounce) can lima beans, drained
1   (14½-ounce) can no-salt-added cut green beans, drained
1   (14½-ounce) can cut wax beans, drained
1   cup chopped red or green bell pepper (about 1 large)
1   cup chopped red onion (about 1 small)
1   cup chopped celery (about 3 large stalks)
1   cup cider vinegar
⅓   cup sugar
½   teaspoon garlic powder
½   teaspoon salt
½   teaspoon freshly ground black pepper

Combine first 7 ingredients in a large bowl; set aside.
Combine vinegar and remaining 4 ingredients in a small saucepan; cook over medium-high heat until mixture comes to a boil and sugar dissolves, stirring occasionally. Pour hot vinegar mixture over bean mixture; toss gently to combine.
Cover and chill at least 8 hours, tossing occasionally. Serve with a slotted spoon.
Yield: 8 servings (serving size: 1 cup).

Per Serving: Calories **118** Fat **0.4g** (sat **0.1g**) Protein **4.5g** Carbohydrate **26.2g** Fiber **4.0g**
Cholesterol **0mg** Iron **2.1mg** Sodium **471mg** Calcium **45mg**
Exchanges: 1 Starch, 1 Vegetable

• make ahead • vegetarian •

Black Bean-Rice Salad

prep: 5 minutes   cook: 7 minutes   chill: 30 minutes

Assembly of this salad is quick and easy. To get great flavor and consistency, allow enough time for it to chill.

1   (16-ounce) package frozen rice pilaf with vegetables
1   (15-ounce) can black beans, rinsed and drained
3   tablespoons reduced-fat olive oil vinaigrette
1   tablespoon lemon juice
¼   teaspoon hot sauce
¼   teaspoon salt
⅛   teaspoon pepper

Cook pilaf according to package directions, omitting salt and fat.
Transfer rice pilaf to a large bowl. Add beans and remaining ingredients to rice pilaf; toss mixture well. Cover and chill 30 minutes.
Yield: 4 servings (serving size: 1 cup).

Per Serving: Calories **205**   Fat **3.2g** (sat **0.1g**)   Protein **7.9g**   Carbohydrate **38.4g**   Fiber **4.3g**
Cholesterol **0mg**   Iron **1.5mg**   Sodium **397mg**   Calcium **16mg**
Exchanges: 2 Starch, 1 Vegetable, ½ Fat

• vegetarian •

Vegetarian Taco Salad

prep: 12 minutes

A complete one-dish meal, this taco salad is chock-full of vegetables, beans, cheese, and tortilla chips.

1   (16-ounce) can kidney beans, rinsed and drained
1   (8¾-ounce) can no-salt-added whole-kernel corn, drained
1   (4.5-ounce) can chopped green chiles, undrained
1   cup chopped tomato (about 1 medium)
½   cup reduced-fat sour cream
¼   cup chopped green onions (about 2)
1   tablespoon 40%-less-sodium taco seasoning
5   cups shredded mixed salad greens
1   (6-ounce) bag nacho-flavored baked tortilla chips (about 6 cups)
½   cup (2 ounces) preshredded fat-free Cheddar cheese

Combine first 7 ingredients in a large bowl; stir well. Add salad greens, and toss gently to coat.
To serve, divide tortilla chips evenly among each of 4 serving plates. Top each serving evenly with salad mixture, and sprinkle with 2 table-spoons cheese.
Yield: 4 servings.

Per Serving: Calories **390**   Fat **10.7g** (sat **3.6g**)   Protein **16.1g**   Carbohydrate **62.8g**   Fiber **9.1g**
Cholesterol **15mg**   Iron **2.1mg**   Sodium **965mg**   Calcium **362mg**
Exchanges: 4 Starch, 1 Vegetable, 1 Fat

• vegetarian •

Mixed Antipasto Salad

prep: 15 minutes

Look for convenient 16-ounce packages of torn romaine lettuce in the produce section of your supermarket.

4	cups torn romaine lettuce
1½	cups sliced mushrooms
⅓	cup sliced red onion (about ½ small)
¼	cup sliced ripe olives
½	cup (2 ounces) part-skim mozzarella cheese, cut into cubes
1	(14-ounce) can artichoke hearts, drained and quartered
1	(7-ounce) bottle roasted red bell peppers, drained and coarsely chopped
¼	cup fat-free Italian dressing
¼	teaspoon coarsely ground black pepper

Combine first 7 ingredients in a large bowl. Add dressing; toss well. Sprinkle with pepper.

Yield: 5 servings (serving size: 1½ cups).

Per Serving: Calories 93 Fat **2.8g** (sat **1.3g**) Protein **5.9g** Carbohydrate **12.9g** Fiber **1.5g**
Cholesterol **7mg** Iron **1.7mg** Sodium **510mg** Calcium **118mg**
Exchanges: 2 Vegetable, ½ Fat

Greek Vegetable-Rotini Salad

prep: 15 minutes   chill: 1 hour

If you increase the variety of foods you eat, you'll create a healthy diet.
Start with this flavorful pasta salad which contains plenty of different
good-for-you foods.

4   ounces uncooked tricolored rotini (corkscrew pasta)
1⅓   cups chopped seeded tomato (about 1 large)
¼   cup finely chopped red onion (about ½ small)
⅔   cup thinly sliced green bell pepper (about 1 small)
12   kalamata olives
⅓   cup (1⅓ ounces) crumbled feta cheese with basil and sun-dried
       tomatoes
2   tablespoons chopped fresh basil
¼   teaspoon freshly ground black pepper
3   tablespoons fat-free balsamic vinaigrette

Cook pasta according to package directions, omitting salt and fat;
drain. Rinse pasta under cold water; drain and set aside.
Combine tomato, onion, and bell pepper; add to pasta. Stir in olives
and next 3 ingredients. Add vinaigrette; toss gently to coat. Cover and
chill 1 hour.
Yield: 6 servings (serving size: ¾ cup).

Per Serving: Calories **113** Fat **2.5g** (sat **1.1g**) Protein **3.8g** Carbohydrate **19.2g** Fiber **1.4g**
Cholesterol **5mg** Iron **1.3mg** Sodium **154mg** Calcium **43mg**
Exchanges: 1 Starch, 1 Vegetable, ½ Fat

Ginger-Peanut Slaw

prep: 10 minutes

This simple slaw is loaded with cruciferous vegetables such as bok choy and red cabbage, which may reduce the risk of cancer.

2½ tablespoons cider vinegar
2½ tablespoons sugar
2 tablespoons low-sodium soy sauce
1 teaspoon grated peeled fresh ginger
¼ cup unsalted, dry-roasted peanuts, toasted
1½ cups shredded bok choy
1¼ cups thinly sliced red cabbage

Combine first 4 ingredients in a small bowl; stir well with a whisk. Set aside.
Combine peanuts, bok choy, and cabbage in a medium bowl; add dressing, and toss gently to coat. Serve with a slotted spoon.
Yield: 4 servings (serving size: ⅔ cup).

Per Serving: Calories **100** Fat **4.6g** (sat **0.6g**) Protein **3.6g** Carbohydrate **13.1g** Fiber **1.7g** Cholesterol **0mg** Iron **0.7mg** Sodium **264mg** Calcium **54mg**
Exchanges: ½ Starch, 1 Vegetable, 1 Fat

Chunky Asian Slaw

prep: 14 minutes

You'll find hoisin sauce in the Asian section of the supermarket. Or you can make your own: Just combine 3 tablespoons brown sugar, 3 tablespoons low-sodium soy sauce, and ¼ teaspoon garlic powder.

4   cups coarsely shredded napa (Chinese) cabbage
1   cup sugar snap peas, cut in half
⅓   cup thinly sliced red bell pepper (½ small)
¼   cup diagonally sliced green onions (about 2)
2   tablespoons rice vinegar
1   tablespoon hoisin sauce
½   teaspoon dark sesame oil
2   tablespoons chopped unsalted, dry-roasted peanuts

Combine first 4 ingredients in a large bowl.
Combine vinegar, hoisin sauce, and oil, stirring well. Pour vinegar mixture over cabbage mixture; toss well.
Serve immediately; or cover and chill. Sprinkle with peanuts just before serving.
Yield: 5 servings (serving size: 1 cup).

Per Serving: Calories **53**   Fat **2.4g** (sat **0.3g**)   Protein **2.3g**   Carbohydrate **6.6g**   Fiber **1.6g**
Cholesterol **0mg**   Iron **1.1mg**   Sodium **134mg**   Calcium **58mg**
Exchanges: 1 Vegetable, ½ Fat

• make ahead • vegetarian •

Sweet-and-Tangy Marinated Slaw

prep: 4 minutes   cook: 2 minutes   chill: 8 hours

Use preshredded broccoli slaw mix, found in the produce section of your supermarket, to get you out of the kitchen fast.

1   (16-ounce) package broccoli slaw mix
½   cup sugar
¼   cup cider vinegar
1   teaspoon prepared mustard
½   teaspoon celery seeds
¼   teaspoon salt
¼   teaspoon pepper
Additional pepper (optional)

Place broccoli slaw in a large bowl. Combine sugar and next 5 ingredients in a small saucepan; bring to a boil. Remove from heat; pour over slaw, and toss well.

Cover; chill 8 hours or overnight. Serve with a slotted spoon. Sprinkle with additional pepper, if desired.

Yield: 5 servings (serving size: 1 cup).

Per Serving: Calories **101**   Fat **0.1g** (sat **0.0g**)   Protein **0.6g**   Carbohydrate **23.9g**   Fiber **1.1g**
Cholesterol **0mg**   Iron **0.3mg**   Sodium **146mg**   Calcium **14mg**
Exchanges: ½ Starch, 2 Vegetable

side
dishes

Maple-Glazed Apples

prep: 5 minutes   cook: 30 minutes

*An apple a day may keep cancer at bay, according to recent research.
Apples contain antioxidant nutrients that may help reduce cancer risk.
They're also an excellent source of fiber, which has been found to
reduce cholesterol and may prevent certain types of cancer.*

$\frac{1}{3}$ cup maple syrup
$\frac{1}{2}$ teaspoon ground cinnamon
$\frac{1}{4}$ teaspoon ground allspice
$\frac{1}{3}$ cup dried cherries
$\frac{1}{2}$ teaspoon vanilla extract
$\frac{1}{4}$ cup chopped pecans
Cooking spray
4   Golden Delicious apples, peeled, cored, and cut into wedges

Combine first 6 ingredients in a small bowl; set aside.
Coat a large nonstick skillet with cooking spray; add apple. Pour syrup
mixture over apple; stir well to coat completely. Cover and cook over
medium heat 30 minutes or until apples are tender, stirring occasionally.
Yield: 4 servings (serving size: $\frac{2}{3}$ cup).

Per Serving: Calories **214**   Fat **5.8g** (sat **0.5g**)   Protein **1.6g**   Carbohydrate **41.0g**   Fiber **4.5g**
Cholesterol **0mg**   Iron **0.9mg**   Sodium **5mg**   Calcium **38mg**
Exchanges: 1 Starch, 1½ Fruit, 1 Fat

Cranberry-Glazed Oranges

prep: 6 minutes   cook: 9 minutes

This holiday side dish can double as dessert. Serve with roasted turkey breast, steamed green beans, and whole wheat rolls.

2 tablespoons sliced almonds
4 navel oranges (about 2½ pounds)
1 (8-ounce) can jellied cranberry sauce
¼ cup orange juice
¼ teaspoon ground cinnamon

Place a large nonstick skillet over medium-high heat. Add almonds, and sauté 5 minutes or until toasted. Remove from pan, and set aside.
Peel oranges, and cut crosswise into ¼-inch-thick slices. Set aside.
Combine cranberry sauce, orange juice, and cinnamon in a bowl, stirring well with a whisk until smooth. Combine cranberry mixture and half of orange slices in pan. Cook over medium heat 2 minutes or until oranges are thoroughly heated, stirring gently. Remove oranges from pan, using a slotted spoon; set aside, and keep warm. Repeat procedure with remaining orange slices.
Place orange slices and any remaining cranberry mixture in a large serving bowl; sprinkle with toasted almonds. Serve immediately.
Yield: 6 servings.

Per Serving: Calories **135** Fat **1.2g** (sat **0.1g**) Protein **1.9g** Carbohydrate **31.0g** Fiber **6.5g** Cholesterol **0mg** Iron **0.3mg** Sodium **19mg** Calcium **62mg**
Exchanges: 2 Fruit

• vegetarian •

Curried Baked Pineapple

prep: 6 minutes   cook: 10 minutes

We used I Can't Believe It's Not Butter! brand butter spray; it adds the taste of butter, but without calories, fat, or cholesterol. You'll find it in your supermarket's dairy case. Serve with roasted chicken and stir-fried green and red bell peppers.

2   (20-ounce) cans pineapple chunks in juice, drained
15   reduced-fat round buttery crackers (such as Ritz), crushed
¼   cup packed brown sugar
¼   cup (1 ounce) preshredded reduced-fat sharp Cheddar cheese
½   teaspoon curry powder
Fat-free butter spray (I Can't Believe It's Not Butter!)

Preheat oven to 450°.
Place pineapple chunks in an ungreased 11 x 7-inch baking dish; set aside.
Combine cracker crumbs and next 3 ingredients, stirring well. Sprinkle cracker mixture over pineapple. Coat cracker mixture with butter spray (about 5 sprays). Bake at 450° for 10 minutes or until lightly browned.
Yield: 8 servings (serving size: about ¾ cup).

Per Serving: Calories **118**   Fat **1.4g** (sat **0.4g**)   Protein **1.4g**   Carbohydrate **24.6g**   Fiber **0.0g**
Cholesterol **2mg**   Iron **0.4mg**   Sodium **82mg**   Calcium **47mg**
Exchanges: ½ Starch, 1 Fruit

Asparagus Spears with Garlic Aïoli

prep: 5 minutes   cook: 3 minutes

When shopping for asparagus, choose firm, pencil-thin spears that are uniform in size with tightly closed bright-green and lavender-tinted tips. Uniformity in size and shape is important for even cooking.

⅓ cup plain low-fat yogurt
1½ tablespoons light mayonnaise
1   teaspoon Dijon mustard
2   garlic cloves, minced
⅛ teaspoon salt
1   pound asparagus spears
Paprika

Combine first 5 ingredients in a small bowl, stirring well with a whisk. Set aside.

Snap off tough ends of asparagus; remove scales from stalks with a knife or a vegetable peeler, if desired.

Place asparagus spears in a large skillet; add water to cover. Bring to a boil over high heat; cover, reduce heat, and simmer 3 minutes or until asparagus is crisp-tender. Plunge asparagus into cold water to stop the cooking process; drain. Place asparagus on a serving platter; spoon yogurt mixture over asparagus. Sprinkle with paprika.

Yield: 4 servings.

Per Serving: Calories **51** Fat **2.2g** (sat **0.6g**) Protein **3.3g** Carbohydrate **5.8g** Fiber **0.8g**
Cholesterol **3mg** Iron **0.6mg** Sodium **175mg** Calcium **56mg**
Exchanges: 1 Vegetable, ½ Fat

Sesame Asparagus and Mushrooms

prep: 5 minutes   cook: 10 minutes

Use the heaviest jelly roll pan or roasting pan available for roasting the vegetables. This is a good side dish to serve with broiled fish and garlic bread.

2   tablespoons rice wine vinegar
1   teaspoon dark sesame oil
1/4 teaspoon salt
1/8 teaspoon garlic powder
1/8 teaspoon freshly ground black pepper
1   pound asparagus spears
1   (8-ounce) package mushrooms
1/2 teaspoon sesame seeds (optional)

Preheat oven to 500°.

Combine first 5 ingredients in a heavy-duty zip-top plastic bag.

Snap off tough ends of asparagus. Remove scales with a knife or vegetable peeler, if desired. Cut asparagus spears in half. Cut mushrooms into quarters (or in half, if small). Add asparagus, mushrooms, and sesame seeds, if desired, to vinegar mixture; seal bag, and turn to coat vegetables well.

Place vegetables in a single layer on a 15 x 10-inch jelly roll pan. Bake at 500° for 10 minutes or until tender, stirring after 5 minutes.

Yield: 6 servings.

Per Serving: Calories **31** Fat **1.3g** (sat **0.2g**) Protein **2.0g** Carbohydrate **4.1g** Fiber **1.5g**
Cholesterol **0mg** Iron **1.0mg** Sodium **101mg** Calcium **18mg**
Exchange: 1 Vegetable

Mexican Black Beans *(photo, page 10)*

prep: 4 minutes   cook: 10 minutes

Slice green onions using kitchen scissors; you won't have to clean a cutting board. Serve these beans with beef fajitas and pineapple wedges.

2   (15-ounce) cans fat-free, no-salt-added black beans, rinsed and
      drained
1   (14.5-ounce) can Mexican-style stewed tomatoes with jalapeño
      peppers and spices, undrained
1   tablespoon red wine vinegar
1   teaspoon sugar
¼   cup sliced green onions (about 2 large)

Combine first 4 ingredients in a large saucepan, stirring well. Cook over medium heat 10 minutes, stirring occasionally. Ladle beans into serving bowls; sprinkle each serving evenly with sliced green onions.
Yield: 7 servings (serving size: 1 cup).

Per Serving: Calories **120**   Fat **0.5g** (sat **0.1g**)   Protein **7.3g**   Carbohydrate **22.1g**   Fiber **4.3g**
Cholesterol **0mg**   Iron **1.7mg**   Sodium **407mg**   Calcium **24mg**
Exchanges: 1½ Starch

Broccoli with Garlic and Lemon-Pepper Sauce

prep: 5 minutes   cook: 10 minutes

Broccoli is one of the best foods you can put on your plate. Phytochemicals in broccoli help to protect your cells' DNA from harmful free radicals.

1   pound broccoli
3   tablespoons light butter
2   to 3 garlic cloves, minced
3   tablespoons lemon juice
1½ tablespoons white wine Worcestershire sauce
⅓   cup water
1   tablespoon Dijon mustard
¼   teaspoon salt
⅛   teaspoon crushed red pepper

Steam broccoli, covered, 7 minutes or until crisp-tender. Transfer to a serving bowl, and keep warm.
Melt butter in a large nonstick skillet over medium-high heat; add garlic. Sauté garlic 1 minute or until golden. Add lemon juice and remaining 5 ingredients; bring to a boil. Pour over broccoli; toss gently. Serve immediately.
Yield: 4 servings.

Per Serving: Calories **86**   Fat **5.2g** (sat **3.1g**)   Protein **4.7g**   Carbohydrate **8.9g**   Fiber **3.1g**
Cholesterol **15mg**   Iron **1.3mg**   Sodium **372mg**   Calcium **61mg**
Exchanges: 2 Vegetable, 1 Fat

Sugared Carrots

prep: 7 minutes   cook: 6 minutes

Carrots are a nutrition powerhouse, prized for the beta-carotene and lutein they contain. Beta-carotene protects the body's cells, and lutein helps preserve eyesight.

1   pound carrots, scraped and cut into ⅛-inch-thick diagonal slices
2   tablespoons brown sugar
1   tablespoon light butter, melted
¼   teaspoon ground nutmeg
¼   teaspoon vanilla extract
⅛   teaspoon salt

Steam carrot, covered, 6 minutes or until crisp-tender. Transfer to a serving bowl, and keep warm.

Combine brown sugar and remaining 4 ingredients in a small bowl. Drizzle over carrot; toss well.

Yield: 4 servings (serving size: ½ cup).

Per Serving: Calories **71** Fat **1.7g** (sat **1.1g**) Protein **1.2g** Carbohydrate **13.9g** Fiber **2.8g**
Cholesterol **5mg** Iron **0.6mg** Sodium **125mg** Calcium **29mg**
Exchanges: 2 Vegetable

Skillet Poblano Corn *(photo, back cover)*

prep: 5 minutes   cook: 5 minutes

Cooking the corn and pepper in batches allows them to have plenty of room in the skillet so they'll develop a savory smoked flavor.

Cooking spray
4   teaspoons light butter, divided
1   cup chopped seeded poblano chile peppers, divided
         (about 2)
3   cups frozen whole-kernel corn, thawed and divided
1   teaspoon ground cumin, divided
½   teaspoon salt

Coat a large nonstick skillet with cooking spray; add 2 teaspoons butter, and melt over medium-high heat. Add ½ cup chopped chiles, and sauté 3 minutes or until tender. Add 1½ cups corn and ½ teaspoon cumin; sauté 2 minutes. Transfer corn mixture to a large serving bowl; cover and keep warm.

Repeat procedure with remaining ingredients. Add to reserved corn mixture. Sprinkle with salt, and toss.

Yield: 5 servings (serving size: ½ cup).

Per Serving: Calories **83**   Fat **2.2g** (sat **1.1g**)   Protein **2.5g**   Carbohydrate **16.5g**   Fiber **2.2g**
Cholesterol **5mg**   Iron **0.8mg**   Sodium **259mg**   Calcium **11mg**
Exchanges: 1 Starch, ½ Fat

Stewed Okra, Corn, and Tomatoes

prep: 3 minutes   cook: 14 minutes

All you do is dump and cook this supereasy recipe. While the vegetables cook, you can cook the bacon in the microwave; it takes 2 to 3 minutes for 3 slices. Serve with broiled shrimp and rice.

1   (16-ounce) package frozen vegetable gumbo mixture
1   (14.5-ounce) can Cajun-style stewed tomatoes with pepper,
        garlic, and Cajun spices
¼   teaspoon no-salt-added Creole seasoning
3   turkey-bacon slices, cooked and crumbled

Combine first 3 ingredients in a large saucepan, stirring well. Cover and cook over medium heat 14 minutes or until vegetables are tender. Sprinkle evenly with crumbled bacon.
Yield: 5 servings (serving size: about 1 cup).

Per Serving: Calories **85**   Fat **1.2g** (sat **0.3g**)   Protein **3.1g**   Carbohydrate **15.9g**   Fiber **3.8g**
Cholesterol **6mg**   Iron **0.0mg**   Sodium **478mg**   Calcium **0mg**
Exchange: 1 Starch

Sugar Snap Peas with Cashews

prep: 5 minutes   cook: 5 minutes

If you can't find frozen sugar snap peas, use frozen snow peas. Serve with chicken teriyaki and rice.

¼   cup orange juice
2   tablespoons low-sodium soy sauce
1½ teaspoons cornstarch
Cooking spray
1   (16-ounce) package frozen sugar snap peas
½   cup thinly sliced green onions (about 4 large)
2   tablespoons chopped salted cashews
Orange slices (optional)

Combine first 3 ingredients, stirring well. Set aside.
Heat a large nonstick skillet coated with cooking spray over medium-high heat. Add peas and green onions, and cook 4 minutes, stirring often. Add orange juice mixture to pan. Cook, stirring constantly, 1 to 2 minutes or until mixture thickens. Transfer to a serving bowl; sprinkle with cashews. Garnish with orange slices, if desired.
Yield: 4 servings.

Per Serving: Calories **97**   Fat **2.9g** (sat **0.5g**)   Protein **4.5g**   Carbohydrate **14.2g**   Fiber **3.5g**
Cholesterol **0mg**   Iron **3.0mg**   Sodium **282mg**   Calcium **60mg**
Exchanges: 1 Starch, ½ Fat

New Potatoes in Seasoned Butter

prep: 5 minutes   cook: 6 minutes

We intentionally left the peel on the potatoes for added flavor and fiber.

1   pound unpeeled small red potatoes, quartered
1   tablespoon light butter
1½ teaspoons lime juice
¾   teaspoon paprika
½   teaspoon salt
3   tablespoons chopped fresh parsley

Steam potatoes, covered, 6 minutes or until tender. Transfer to a large serving bowl, and keep warm.
Combine butter and next 3 ingredients in a small bowl; stir well. Add to potatoes, and toss gently. Sprinkle potatoes with parsley, and toss again. Serve immediately.
Yield: 4 servings (serving size: about ⅔ cup).

Per Serving: Calories **105**   Fat **1.7g** (sat **1.0g**)   Protein **2.8g**   Carbohydrate **21.0g**   Fiber **2.0g**
Cholesterol **5mg**   Iron **1.1mg**   Sodium **319mg**   Calcium **13mg**
Exchanges: 1½ Starch

Mashed Parsley Potatoes

prep: 5 minutes   cook: 9 minutes

An easy way to chop fresh parsley is to pack it in a measuring cup and snip it with kitchen scissors until it's chopped. Serve these potatoes with meat loaf and steamed green beans.

1   pound unpeeled red potatoes (small to medium size)
2   tablespoons water
¼   cup fat-free milk
1½ tablespoons reduced-calorie stick margarine
1   tablespoon chopped fresh parsley
½   teaspoon seasoned salt
⅛   teaspoon pepper

Cut potatoes into quarters; place potato and water in a medium-sized microwave-safe bowl. Cover tightly with heavy-duty plastic wrap; fold back a small edge of wrap to allow steam to escape. Microwave at HIGH 9 minutes or until tender, stirring after 4 minutes.
Drain potato; return to bowl. Add milk and remaining ingredients. Mash with a potato masher or fork until potato is mashed and mixture is combined.
Yield: 4 servings (serving size: ½ cup).

Per Serving: Calories **113** Carbohydrate **19.8g** Fat **2.9g** (sat **0.4g**) Fiber **2.1g** Protein **3.1g**
Cholesterol **0mg** Sodium **305mg** Calcium **35mg** Iron **1.6mg**
Exchanges: 1½ Starch, ½ Fat

Roasted Sweet Potatoes and Onions

prep: 10 minutes   cook: 20 minutes

Sweet potatoes are one of nature's most nutrient-dense foods. Loaded with fiber, vitamin C, and especially beta-carotene, sweet potatoes are among the top good-for-you foods.

1   large sweet potato, peeled and cut into ½-inch cubes
1   onion, cut into ½-inch wedges
2   teaspoons extravirgin olive oil
¼   teaspoon salt
⅛   teaspoon pepper
Cooking spray

Preheat oven to 400°.
Combine first 5 ingredients in a large bowl; toss well.
Coat a nonstick baking sheet with cooking spray; add potato mixture, and arrange in a single layer.
Bake at 400° for 20 to 25 minutes or until potato is tender, stirring once. Serve immediately.

Yield: 4 servings (serving size: ½ cup).

Per Serving: Calories **121** Fat **2.6g** (sat **0.4g**) Protein **1.8g** Carbohydrate **23.2g** Fiber **2.2g**
Cholesterol **0mg** Iron **0.6mg** Sodium **158mg** Calcium **26mg**
Exchanges: 1½ Starch, ½ Fat

Creamed Spinach

prep: 5 minutes   cook: 14 minutes

To make your own garlic-flavored light cream cheese, use plain light cream cheese and stir in ⅛ teaspoon garlic powder. Serve with pork loin chops and steamed carrots.

1   (10-ounce) package frozen chopped spinach
3   tablespoons roasted garlic-flavored light cream cheese
Cooking spray
¼   cup chopped onion (about ¼ small)
¼   cup chopped red bell pepper (about ¼ small)
¼   teaspoon salt
Dash of black pepper
¾   cup evaporated fat-free milk

Cook spinach according to package directions, omitting salt; drain well. Combine spinach and cream cheese in a bowl, stirring well.
Heat a medium saucepan coated with cooking spray over medium-high heat. Add onion and red bell pepper, and cook 3 minutes until tender, stirring often. Stir in spinach mixture, salt, and black pepper.
Reduce heat to medium-low. Gradually add milk, stirring until smooth. Cook, stirring constantly, 3 to 5 minutes or until mixture is creamy.
Yield: 3 servings.

Per Serving: Calories **117** Fat **3.2g** (sat **1.9g**) Protein **9.3g** Carbohydrate **13.7g** Fiber **3.4g** Cholesterol **10mg** Iron **2.3mg** Sodium **430mg** Calcium **294mg**
Exchanges: 2 Vegetable, ½ Skim Milk, ½ Fat

• vegetarian •

Cheese-Stuffed Tomatoes

prep: 13 minutes   cook: 12 minutes

This delicious side dish is elegant enough to serve to company.

4   small firm, ripe tomatoes
2   tablespoons fat-free balsamic vinaigrette
16 small basil leaves
2   (1-ounce) slices part-skim mozzarella cheese, cut into 8 (2-inch)
      squares
1   teaspoon Italian-seasoned breadcrumbs
¼   teaspoon freshly ground black pepper

Preheat oven to 350°.
Cut a ⅛-inch-thick slice off bottom of each tomato (so tomato will sit
flat in baking dish). Remove stem portion from top of tomato.
Cut each tomato horizontally into thirds. Place 4 bottom tomato slices
in an 11 x 7-inch baking dish; brush evenly with 2 teaspoons vinaigrette.
Top each with 2 basil leaves and a cheese slice. Repeat layers.
Top with remaining 4 tomato slices; brush with remaining 2 teaspoons
vinaigrette. Sprinkle evenly with breadcrumbs and pepper. Bake at
350° for 12 minutes or until cheese melts. Serve tomatoes immediately.
Yield: 4 servings.

Per Serving: Calories **66** Fat **2.6g** (sat **1.5g**) Protein **4.4g** Carbohydrate **7.1g** Fiber **1.3g**
Cholesterol **8mg** Iron **0.5mg** Sodium **191mg** Calcium **98mg**
Exchanges: 1½ Vegetable, ½ Fat

Lemon Pasta

prep: 5 minutes   cook: 12 minutes

There will be excess liquid in the skillet when you first add the mushroom mixture, but the pasta absorbs a good bit of it, leaving the pasta well coated. Serve with grilled fish and a spinach salad.

6   ounces uncooked penne (tube-shaped pasta)
1   teaspoon garlic-flavored olive oil
1½ cups sliced mushrooms
⅓   cup sliced green onions (about 3 medium)
½   cup dry white wine
½   to 1 teaspoon grated lemon rind
¼   teaspoon salt
½   teaspoon lemon pepper seasoning

Cook pasta according to package directions, omitting salt and fat; drain well.

While pasta cooks, add olive oil to a large nonstick skillet; place over medium-high heat. Add mushrooms and green onions, and cook 3 minutes, stirring often. Add wine; cook 5 minutes or until wine is reduced by half. Pour mushroom mixture over pasta; add lemon rind, salt, and lemon pepper seasoning. Toss well. Serve immediately.

Yield: 6 servings (serving size: about ¾ cup).

Per Serving: Calories **118**   Fat **1.3g** (sat **0.2g**)   Protein **4.1g**   Carbohydrate **22.5g**   Fiber **1.0g**
Cholesterol **0mg**   Iron **1.4mg**   Sodium **137mg**   Calcium **10mg**
Exchanges: 1½ Starch

Spicy Peanut Pasta *(photo, page 8)*

prep: 5 minutes   cook: 10 minutes

You'll enjoy the distinct combination of Asian flavors—peanut butter, soy sauce, and red bell pepper—in this creamy pasta side dish.

6	ounces uncooked vermicelli
1	(16-ounce) package frozen sugar snap pea stir-fry mix
¼	cup reduced-fat crunchy peanut butter
3	tablespoons rice wine vinegar
3	tablespoons low-sodium soy sauce
2	teaspoons sugar
2	teaspoons sesame oil
½	to 1 teaspoon red bell pepper flakes
3	tablespoons diagonally sliced green onions (about 1)

Cook pasta according to package directions, omitting salt and fat. Add sugar snap pea mix for the last 4 minutes of cooking time. Drain pasta mixture, and place in a serving bowl; keep warm.

While pasta cooks, combine peanut butter and next 5 ingredients in a small saucepan. Cook over medium heat until peanut butter melts, stirring often. Add to pasta mixture; toss well. Sprinkle with green onions. Serve immediately.

Yield: 10 servings (serving size: ½ cup).

Per Serving: Calories **151**   Fat **3.8g** (sat **0.7g**)   Protein **6.4g**   Carbohydrate **23.3g**   Fiber **2.9g**
Cholesterol **0mg**   Iron **5.5mg**   Sodium **243mg**   Calcium **15mg**
Exchanges: 1½ Starch, ½ Fat

• vegetarian •

Quick Spanish Rice

prep: 3 minutes   cook: 5 minutes

Frozen seasoning blend is a mix of chopped onions, celery, red bell peppers, green bell peppers, and parsley. It's handy to use in soups, stews, and sauces, too. Serve with baked chicken quesadillas and a fruit salad.

1	cup water
1	(8-ounce) can no-salt-added tomato sauce
¾	cup frozen onion and pepper seasoning blend (such as McKenzie's)
½	cup thick and chunky salsa
½	teaspoon chili powder
¼	teaspoon salt
2	cups instant rice, uncooked

Combine first 6 ingredients in a medium saucepan; bring to a boil. Stir in rice. Cover, remove from heat, and let stand 5 minutes or until liquid is absorbed and rice is tender.

Yield: 8 servings (serving size: about ¾ cup).

Per Serving: Calories **108**   Fat **0.1g** (sat **0.0g**)   Protein **2.5g**   Carbohydrate **23.8g**   Fiber **0.7g**   Cholesterol **0mg**   Iron **1.1mg**   Sodium **128mg**   Calcium **12mg**
Exchanges: 1½ Starch

Rice with Black-Eyed Peas

prep: 3 minutes   cook: 5 minutes   stand: 5 minutes

A one-cup serving makes a satisfying meatless main dish with 238 calories.

Cooking spray
1   teaspoon vegetable oil
1½ cups frozen onion and pepper seasoning blend (such as
       McKenzie's)
1   teaspoon minced garlic
1½ cups fat-free, less-sodium chicken broth
1   teaspoon dried thyme
¼   teaspoon salt
1½ cups instant rice, uncooked
1   (15.8-ounce) can black-eyed peas, rinsed and drained
1   teaspoon hot sauce

Coat a large saucepan with cooking spray, and add oil. Place over
medium-high heat. Add seasoning blend and garlic; sauté 4 minutes.
Add broth, thyme, and salt to seasoning blend mixture. Bring to a boil.
Add rice, stirring well.
Cover, remove from heat, and let stand 5 minutes or until liquid is
absorbed and rice is tender. Stir in peas and hot sauce. Serve immediately.
Yield: 8 servings (serving size: ½ cup).

Per Serving: Calories **119**   Fat **1.1g** (sat **0.2g**)   Protein **4.9g**   Carbohydrate **21.8g**   Fiber **0.9g**
Cholesterol **0mg**   Iron **1.4mg**   Sodium **243mg**   Calcium **17mg**
Exchanges: 1½ Starch

Mushroom Barley *(photo, page 10)*

prep: 5 minutes   cook: 13 minutes   stand: 5 minutes

Look for barley on the same aisle in the supermarket as rice and other grains. Serve with grilled flank steak and roasted yellow and zucchini squash.

1   (14¼-ounce) can no-salt-added beef broth
1   tablespoon low-sodium Worcestershire sauce
¼   teaspoon salt
¼   teaspoon freshly ground black pepper
1   cup uncooked quick-cooking barley
Cooking spray
1   (8-ounce) package presliced mushrooms
¾   cup frozen chopped onion, thawed
½   cup finely chopped celery (about 1 stalk)

Combine first 4 ingredients in a medium saucepan; bring to a boil. Add barley; cover, reduce heat, and simmer 10 minutes. Remove from heat, and let stand 5 minutes.

While barley stands, heat a large nonstick skillet coated with cooking spray over medium-high heat. Add mushrooms, onion, and celery; cook 3 minutes or until tender, stirring often. Stir into cooked barley.

Yield: 8 servings (serving size: about ½ cup).

Per Serving: Calories **109**   Fat **0.5g** (sat **0.1g**)   Protein **3.4g**   Carbohydrate **23.0g**   Fiber **4.7g**
Cholesterol **0mg**   Iron **1.1mg**   Sodium **93mg**   Calcium **15mg**
Exchanges: 1½ Starch

Mediterranean Couscous

prep: 8 minutes   cook: 5 minutes

Vary the flavor slightly in this recipe by using a flavored feta cheese with basil and sun-dried tomatoes or peppercorns.

1   (5.8-ounce) package roasted garlic and olive oil couscous mix
1   (14-ounce) can artichoke hearts, drained and chopped
1¼ cups chopped tomato (about 1 large)
½   cup (2 ounces) crumbled feta cheese
¼   cup sliced ripe olives
1   tablespoon chopped fresh parsley
2   tablespoons lemon juice
1   teaspoon dried oregano
¼   teaspoon pepper

Prepare couscous according to package directions, omitting fat and using 1 tablespoon seasoning from seasoning packet; discard remaining seasoning. Fluff couscous with a fork.

Add chopped artichoke and remaining ingredients to couscous; toss gently. Serve warm or chilled.

Yield: 7 servings (serving size: about ¾ cup).

Per Serving: Calories **144**   Fat **3.5g** (sat **1.6g**)   Protein **6.0g**   Carbohydrate **24.1g**   Fiber **1.5g**
Cholesterol **9mg**   Iron **1.1mg**   Sodium **262mg**   Calcium **77mg**
Exchanges: 1½ Starch, ½ Fat

Garlic-Cheese Grits

prep: 9 minutes   cook: 7 minutes

Light processed American cheese melts quickly and makes these grits smooth and creamy.

4   cups water
¼   teaspoon salt
2   large garlic cloves, minced
1   cup uncooked quick-cooking grits
6   ounces light processed American cheese, cubed
½   teaspoon low-sodium Worcestershire sauce
¼   teaspoon dry mustard
⅛   teaspoon ground red pepper

Combine first 3 ingredients in a medium saucepan; bring to a boil. Slowly stir in grits; cover, reduce heat, and simmer 5 minutes or until grits are thickened, stirring occasionally.

Add cheese and remaining ingredients to grits; stir until cheese melts. Serve immediately.

Yield: 6 servings (serving size: about ¾ cup).

Per Serving: Calories **142**   Fat **2.2g** (sat **0.6g**)   Protein **9.3g**   Carbohydrate **21.4g**   Fiber **1.3g**
Cholesterol **0mg**   Iron **0.9mg**   Sodium **507mg**   Calcium **201mg**
Exchanges: 1½ Starch, ½ Medium-Fat Meat

slow cooker

Southwestern Meat Loaf

prep: 15 minutes   cook: 3½ to 8 hours   stand: 10 minutes

This meat loaf recipe is especially good served with Mashed Parsley Potatoes (recipe on page 234). Round out the meal with steamed green beans.

Cooking spray
2   pounds ground round
2   (1.6-ounce) slices light sandwich bread, crumbled (1 cup)
1   cup chopped onion (about 1 medium)
½   cup egg substitute
¼   teaspoon salt
¼   teaspoon freshly ground black pepper
½   cup ketchup
½   cup thick and chunky salsa

Coat a 3½-quart electric slow cooker with cooking spray. Tear off two lengths of aluminum foil long enough to fit in bottom of slow cooker, and extend 3 inches over each side of slow cooker. Fold each foil strip lengthwise to form 2-inch-wide strips. Arrange foil strips in a cross fashion in cooker, pressing strips in bottom of cooker and extending ends over sides of cooker.

Combine beef and next 5 ingredients; shape mixture into a loaf the shape of the slow cooker container. Place loaf in slow cooker over foil strips. (Foil strips become "handles" to remove meat loaf from slow cooker.) Make a shallow indention on top of meat loaf. Combine ketchup and salsa; pour over meat loaf.

Cover with lid, and cook on high-heat setting 3½ to 4 hours. Or cook on high-heat setting 1 hour; reduce to low-heat setting, and cook 7 hours. Use foil strips to lift meat loaf from cooker. Let meat loaf stand 10 minutes before slicing.

Yield: 8 servings (serving size: 1 slice).

Per Serving: Calories 209   Fat **6.0g** (sat **2.1g**)   Protein **27.9g**   Carbohydrate **9.8g**   Fiber **1.1g**
Cholesterol **66mg**   Iron **3.1mg**   Sodium **415mg**   Calcium **31mg**
Exchanges: ½ Starch, 4 Very Lean Meat

Chili Grande

prep: 5 minutes   cook: 4 to 8 hours

Spice up your mealtime with this south-of-the border dinner delight. Serve with tortilla chips, if desired.

¾ pound beef stew meat, trimmed and cut into ½-inch pieces
1   tablespoon salt-free Mexican seasoning
2   (15½-ounce) cans chili beans in zesty sauce, undrained
1   (14.5-ounce) can no-salt-added stewed tomatoes, undrained
1   (10-ounce) package frozen chopped green bell pepper
      (about 3 cups)
1   cup frozen chopped onion

Place all ingredients in a 4- or 5-quart electric slow cooker; stir well. Cover with lid, and cook on high-heat setting 4 hours. Or cover and cook on high-heat setting 1 hour; reduce to low-heat setting, and cook 7 hours.

Yield: 6 servings (serving size: 1½ cups).

Per Serving: Calories **256**   Fat **4.0g** (sat **0.9g**)   Protein **22.9g**   Carbohydrate **38.3g**   Fiber **9.4g**
Cholesterol **32mg**   Iron **3.5mg**   Sodium **722mg**   Calcium **94mg**
Exchanges: 2 Starch, 2 Vegetable, 2 Lean Meat

Mediterranean Beef Stew *(photo, page 5)*

prep: 5 minutes   cook: 5 to 8 hours

The juices from the beef give this velvety stew its richness. Serve with sun-dried tomato bread.

2   zucchini, cut into bite-sized pieces
¾   pound beef stew meat, trimmed and cut into ½-inch pieces
2   (14.5-ounce) cans diced tomatoes with basil, garlic, and oregano, undrained
½   teaspoon pepper
1   (2-inch) cinnamon stick or ¼ teaspoon ground cinnamon

Place zucchini in bottom of a 3½-quart electric slow cooker. Add beef and remaining ingredients. Cover with lid, and cook on high-heat setting 5 hours or until meat is tender. Or cover and cook on high-heat setting 1 hour; reduce to low-heat setting, and cook 7 hours. Remove and discard cinnamon stick before serving.

Yield: 4 servings (serving size: 1½ cups).

Per Serving: Calories **193** Fat **4.0g** (sat **1.3g**) Protein **22.8g** Carbohydrate **16.9g** Fiber **1.5g**
Cholesterol **48mg** Iron **3.5mg** Sodium **572mg** Calcium **123mg**
Exchanges: 1 Starch, 3 Very Lean Meat

Mexican-Style Steak and Beans

prep: 6 minutes   cook: 4 hours

Serve with warm flour tortillas and a romaine salad drizzled with fat-free ranch dressing.

1   (1-pound) flank steak (½ inch thick), trimmed
Cooking spray
1   tablespoon mild Mexican seasoning blend (such as Morton
        & Bassett)
½   teaspoon salt
2   small green bell peppers, cut into thin strips
1   cup frozen chopped onion
1   (10-ounce) can diced tomatoes and green chiles, undrained
1   (15-ounce) can no-salt-added pinto beans, rinsed and drained
3   cups hot cooked rice

Cut steak into 6 even pieces. Place in a 3½- to 4-quart electric slow cooker coated with cooking spray. Sprinkle steak with Mexican seasoning blend and salt. Add green peppers, onion, and tomatoes and green chiles. Cover with lid, and cook on high-heat setting 4 hours, adding pinto beans during the last 30 minutes of cooking. Serve over rice.
Yield: 6 servings.

Per Serving: Calories **335** Fat **7.6g** (sat **3.1g**) Protein **21.7g** Carbohydrate **41.8g** Fiber **5.5g**
Cholesterol **38mg** Iron **3.8mg** Sodium **461mg** Calcium **69mg**
Exchanges: 2 Starch, 2 Vegetable, 2 Lean Meat

Country Steak with Gravy

prep: 8 minutes   cook: 8 hours

Jars of fat-free beef gravy and poultry gravy are great convenience products for low-fat cooking. However, they're higher in sodium than traditional canned or jarred gravies. Serve this down-home dish with rice and glazed carrots.

1   (12-ounce) jar fat-free beef-flavored gravy
1   teaspoon dried thyme
½   teaspoon freshly ground black pepper
¼   teaspoon garlic powder
Cooking spray
1½ pounds boneless top round steak (½ inch thick), trimmed

Place gravy, thyme, pepper, and garlic powder in a 4-quart electric slow cooker coated with cooking spray; stir well.
Cut steak into serving-sized pieces, and add to slow cooker; spoon gravy over steak to completely cover steak. Cover with lid, and cook on high-heat setting 1 hour; reduce to low-heat setting, and cook 7 hours.
Yield: 6 servings.

Per Serving: Calories **165**   Fat **4.7g** (sat **1.7g**)   Protein **26.9g**   Carbohydrate **3.4g**   Fiber **0.1g**
Cholesterol **65mg**   Iron **2.7mg**   Sodium **409mg**   Calcium **9mg**
Exchanges: 4 Very Lean Meat

Home-Style Beef Pot Roast

prep: 13 minutes   cook: 4 to 8 hours

Long, slow cooking tenderizes lean cuts of meat. Other lean roasts you can substitute include round tip and sirloin. Serve with roasted potatoes and carrots.

Cooking spray
1   (3-pound) eye-of-round roast, trimmed
½   teaspoon freshly ground black pepper
1¼ cups water, divided
1   (1-ounce) package brown gravy mix with onions
1   teaspoon cornstarch

Coat a large nonstick skillet with cooking spray; place over medium-high heat. Sprinkle roast on all sides with pepper. Add roast to pan, and cook until browned on all sides; place in a 3½- to 4-quart electric slow cooker coated with cooking spray.

Combine 1 cup water and gravy mix; pour over roast. Cover with lid, and cook on high-heat setting 4 to 5 hours. Or cook on high-heat setting 1 hour; reduce to low-heat setting, and cook 7 to 9 hours. Remove roast from sauce; cover roast, and keep warm.

Combine remaining ¼ cup water and cornstarch, stirring with a whisk until smooth. Slowly stir cornstarch mixture into gravy in slow cooker. Pour mixture into a 1-quart microwave-safe glass measure, stirring until blended. Microwave at HIGH 2 minutes or until thickened, stirring after 1 minute. Serve roast with gravy.

Yield: 12 servings.

Per Serving: Calories **251** Fat **16.4g** (sat **6.5g**) Protein **22.6g** Carbohydrate **1.7g** Fiber **0.1g**
Cholesterol **69mg** Iron **1.6mg** Sodium **170mg** Calcium **9mg**
Exchanges: 3 Medium-Fat Meat

Picante Pork Chops

prep: 7 minutes   cook: 3 to 10 hours

To remove excess fat from the sauce, drop an ice cube into the sauce, and remove the ice with a slotted spoon. The hardened fat will cling to the ice cube. Serve with rice and steamed zucchini.

8   (6-ounce) bone-in center-cut loin pork chops (about ½ inch thick), trimmed
Cooking spray
1   (16-ounce) jar thick and chunky picante sauce

Heat a large skillet coated with cooking spray over medium-high heat. Add chops; cook until browned on both sides.
Pour one-fourth of picante sauce into a 3½- to 4-quart electric slow cooker coated with cooking spray; add chops. Top with remaining picante sauce. Cover with lid, and cook on high-heat setting 3 to 4 hours. Or cook on high-heat setting 1 hour; reduce to low-heat setting, and cook 9 hours. Reserve 1 cup sauce. Serve sauce over chops.

Yield: 8 servings (serving size: 1 chop and 2 tablespoons sauce).

Per Serving: Calories **119**   Fat **4.7g** (sat **1.6g**)   Protein **15.2g**   Carbohydrate **3.0g**   Fiber **0.4g**
Cholesterol **41mg**   Iron **0.5mg**   Sodium **273mg**   Calcium **3mg**
Exchanges: 2 Lean Meat

Cranberry Pork Roast

prep: 15 minutes   cook: 4 to 8 hours

*You don't have to brown the roast before putting it in the slow cooker.
However, browning the outside of the roast adds a rich caramelized flavor
to the meat. Serve with couscous and steamed broccoli.*

Cooking spray
1   (3-pound) boneless pork loin roast, trimmed
1   (16-ounce) can whole-berry cranberry sauce
¼   cup steak sauce
1   tablespoon brown sugar
1   teaspoon prepared mustard
2   tablespoons water
2   tablespoons cornstarch

Coat a large nonstick skillet with cooking spray; place over medium-
high heat. Add roast; cook until browned on all sides. Place roast in a
4- to 5-quart electric slow cooker coated with cooking spray.
Combine cranberry sauce and next 3 ingredients; pour over roast.
Cover with lid, and cook on high-heat setting 4 to 5 hours. Or cook on
high-heat setting 1 hour; reduce to low-heat setting, and cook 7 hours.
Remove roast from sauce; cover and keep warm.
Combine water and cornstarch, stirring with a whisk until smooth.
Slowly stir cornstarch mixture into sauce in slow cooker. Pour mixture
into a 1-quart microwave-safe glass measure. Microwave at HIGH 2
minutes, stirring after 1 minute. Serve roast with gravy.
Yield: 12 servings.

Per Serving: Calories **252**   Fat **9.3g** (sat **3.0g**)   Protein **23.5g**   Carbohydrate **17.0g**   Fiber **0.0g**
Cholesterol **68mg**   Iron **1.1mg**   Sodium **169mg**   Calcium **17mg**
Exchanges: 1 Starch, 3 Lean Meat

Moroccan Chicken and Lentils

prep: 2 minutes   cook: 5 to 8 hours

*Turmeric, a spice used in curries, gives this chicken its Moroccan flavor.
Look for lentils in the rice and dried bean section of the grocery. Serve
with couscous and toasted pita chips.*

½   (16-ounce) package baby carrots
1½ cups dried lentils
1½ pounds frozen chicken breast tenders
2   tablespoons minced garlic
¾   teaspoon salt
2   teaspoons salt-free Moroccan rub (or ¾ teaspoon
      ground turmeric, ½ teaspoon ground red pepper,
      and ½ teaspoon ground cinnamon)
2   (14-ounce) cans fat-free, less-sodium chicken broth

Place all ingredients, in order listed, in a 4- or 5-quart electric slow
cooker. Cover with lid, and cook on high-heat setting 5 hours. Or cover
and cook on high-heat setting 1 hour; reduce to low-heat setting, and
cook 7 hours.

Yield: 6 servings (serving size: 1 cup).

Per Serving: Calories **299**   Fat **2.1g** (sat **0.5g**)   Protein **40.5g**   Carbohydrate **30.2g**   Fiber **10.8g**
Cholesterol **66mg**   Iron **5.5mg**   Sodium **749mg**   Calcium **53mg**
Exchanges: 2 Starch, 1 Vegetable, 4 Very Lean Meat

Hearty Chicken-Sausage Soup

prep: 7 minutes   cook: 4 to 8 hours

Turkey sausage and Cajun-style tomatoes flavor this gumbo-like soup.
Serve with crusty French bread.

1   (16-ounce) package frozen vegetable gumbo mixture
1   pound skinless, boneless chicken breast halves, cut into
        1-inch pieces
4   ounces turkey kielbasa sausage, sliced
1   (14.5-ounce) can Cajun-style stewed tomatoes with pepper,
        garlic, and Cajun spices, undrained
1   (14-ounce) can fat-free, less-sodium chicken broth
2   teaspoons salt-free extraspicy seasoning
2   cups cooked long-grain rice

Place first 6 ingredients in a 3½-quart electric slow cooker; stir well.
Cover with lid, and cook on high-heat setting 4 hours. Or cover and
cook on high-heat setting 1 hour; reduce to low-heat setting, and cook
7 hours. Stir in cooked rice during last 30 minutes of cooking time.
Yield: 6 servings (serving size: 1¼ cups).

Per Serving: Calories **240** Fat **1.6g** (sat **0.4g**) Protein **23.6g** Carbohydrate **30.7g** Fiber **2.6g**
Cholesterol **52mg** Iron **1.6mg** Sodium **471mg** Calcium **68mg**
Exchanges: 2 Starch, 3 Very Lean Meat

Chicken Pepper Pot

prep: 5 minutes   cook: 4 to 8 hours

Put the ingredients in the slow cooker, and head out the door. Serve with rice or noodles and crusty French bread.

2   (16-ounce) packages frozen pepper stir-fry
4   (6-ounce) skinless bone-in chicken breast halves
1   (10¾-ounce) can reduced-fat, reduced-sodium tomato soup with garden herbs
1   tablespoon white wine Worcestershire sauce
½   teaspoon garlic salt

Place all ingredients in a 4- or 5-quart electric slow cooker; stir well. Cover with lid, and cook on high-heat setting 4 hours. Or cover and cook on high-heat setting 1 hour; reduce to low-heat setting, and cook 7 hours.

Yield: 4 servings.

Per Serving: Calories **245**   Fat **2.7g** (sat **0.5g**)   Protein **33.7g**   Carbohydrate **19.2g**   Fiber **3.3g**
Cholesterol **79mg**   Iron **1.9mg**   Sodium **670mg**   Calcium **39mg**
Exchanges: 1 Starch, 1 Vegetable, 4 Very Lean Meat

Chinese Chicken Soup

prep: 8 minutes   cook: 7 hours

Water chestnuts are the health-conscious cook's friend, as they add texture to recipes without excess calories or fat. Serve this Asian-inspired soup with whole wheat rolls and orange sherbet.

1   (15¼-ounce) can pineapple tidbits in juice, undrained
1   (8-ounce) can sliced water chestnuts, undrained
⅓   cup low-sodium soy sauce
¾   to 1 teaspoon Chinese five-spice powder
3   carrots, scraped and sliced
4   green onions, diagonally cut into 2-inch pieces
½   teaspoon salt
½   teaspoon freshly ground black pepper
2   (6-ounce) skinless bone-in chicken breast halves
2   (4-ounce) chicken thighs, skinned

Drain pineapple and water chestnuts, reserving liquids. Add soy sauce and five-spice powder to liquids; stir well.

Place pineapple, water chestnuts, carrot, and green onions in a 3½-quart electric slow cooker. Sprinkle salt and pepper over chicken; place chicken over vegetables. Pour liquid mixture over chicken. Cover with lid, and cook on high-heat setting 1 hour; reduce heat to low-heat setting, and cook 6 hours.

Remove chicken from bones, and shred meat. Add meat to vegetable mixture.

Yield: 4 servings (serving size: 1½ cups).

Per Serving: Calories **185**   Fat **1.8g** (sat **0.4g**)   Protein **14.7g**   Carbohydrate **29.9g**   Fiber **5.8g**
Cholesterol **39mg**   Iron **1.1mg**   Sodium **1,037mg**   Calcium **25mg**
Exchanges: 2½ Vegetable, 1 Fruit, 1½ Very Lean Meat

Fruited Chicken and Barley

prep: 5 minutes   cook: 4 to 8 hours

Slow cooking these thighs all day makes them extratender and juicy.
Serve with steamed green beans and warm multigrain rolls.

1¼ cups uncooked pearl barley
6   cups water
2   pounds chicken thighs, skinned
1   large onion, coarsely chopped
1   (8-ounce) package dried mixed fruit
1   tablespoon salt-free Caribbean spice rub
½   teaspoon salt
¼   teaspoon pepper

Place all ingredients in a 4-quart electric slow cooker; stir well. Cover
with lid, and cook on high-heat setting 4 hours or until chicken is tender.
Or cover and cook on high-heat setting 1 hour; reduce to low-heat
setting, and cook 7 hours.

Yield: 6 servings (serving size: 2 cups).

Per Serving: Calories **399**   Fat **5.2g** (sat **1.3g**)   Protein **28.8g**   Carbohydrate **58.3g**   Fiber **9.7g**
Cholesterol **99mg**   Iron **3.4mg**   Sodium **316mg**   Calcium **44mg**
Exchanges: 3 Starch, 1 Fruit, 3 Very Lean Meat

Glazed Turkey

prep: 3 minutes   cook: 5 to 8 hours

There are usually 2 tenderloins in a package; place the second one in an airtight container, and freeze up to 1 month. Serve with wild rice, apple slices, and whole wheat rolls.

4   sweet potatoes, scrubbed
1   (¾-pound) turkey tenderloin
1   (14-ounce) can fat-free, less-sodium chicken broth
2   bay leaves
½   cup apricot spread (such as Polaner All Fruit)

Place potatoes in bottom of a 5-quart electric slow cooker; place turkey over potatoes.
Pour broth over turkey; add bay leaves and apricot spread. Cover with lid, and cook on high-heat setting 5 hours or until turkey is tender. Or cover and cook on high-heat setting 1 hour; reduce to low-heat setting, and cook 7 hours. Remove and discard bay leaves. Slice and serve tenderloin with potatoes.
Yield: 4 servings.

Per Serving: Calories **342** Fat **1.8g** (sat **0.5g**) Protein **23.2g** Carbohydrate **56.6g** Fiber **5.1g**
Cholesterol **51mg** Iron **2.0mg** Sodium **110mg** Calcium **37mg**
Exchanges: 4 Starch, 2 Very Lean Meat

Chill-Breaker Turkey Chili

prep: 9 minutes   cook: 4 to 8 hours

To save time you can add the ground turkey to the slow cooker without cooking it first. The texture of the cooked turkey will be a bit softer, but we liked it both ways. Serve with Corn Bread (recipe on page 63).

Cooking spray
1   pound ground turkey breast
1   cup frozen chopped onion
1   (8-ounce) can no-salt-added tomato sauce
1   (30-ounce) can chili-hot beans, undrained
1   (1.25-ounce) package mild chili seasoning mix

Coat a Dutch oven with cooking spray; add turkey and onion, and place over high heat. Sauté until turkey crumbles and onion is tender. **Add** tomato sauce, beans, and seasoning mix to turkey mixture; stir well. Pour mixture into a 3½- to 4-quart electric slow cooker coated with cooking spray. Cover and cook on high-heat setting 4 to 5 hours. Or cook on high-heat setting 1 hour; reduce to low-heat setting, and cook 7 to 9 hours.
Yield: 6 servings (serving size: 1 cup).

Per Serving: Calories **268**   Fat **2.5g** (sat **1.0g**)   Protein **21.0g**   Carbohydrate **31.3g**   Fiber **8.0g**
Cholesterol **45mg**   Iron **0.9mg**   Sodium **463mg**   Calcium **13mg**
Exchanges: 2 Starch, 2 Very Lean Meat

soups & sandwiches

Chilled Strawberry-Ginger Soup

prep: 10 minutes   chill: 1 hour

*If you don't have time to peel, chop, or slice raw fruits and vegetables,
reach for frozen and canned foods. For example, you can enjoy this quick
fruit soup year-round with convenient frozen berries and canned pears.*

1   (16-ounce) package frozen unsweetened strawberries,
        partially thawed
1   (15-ounce) can pear halves in juice, undrained
½   cup frozen orange juice concentrate
¼   cup honey
1   tablespoon grated peeled fresh ginger

Place all ingredients in a blender; process until smooth, stopping once
to scrape down sides. Cover and chill 1 hour.

Yield: 6 servings (serving size: ¾ cup).

Per Serving: Calories **143**   Fat **0.2g** (sat **0.0g**)   Protein **1.2g**   Carbohydrate **36.8g**   Fiber **1.4g**
Cholesterol **0mg**   Iron **0.9mg**   Sodium **6mg**   Calcium **27mg**
Exchanges: ½ Starch, 2 Fruit

Tropical Melon Soup

prep: 10 minutes   chill: 1 hour

This simple soup is brimming with the cancer-fighting antioxidant, beta-carotene. This plant pigment isn't only a powerful nutrient, but it also gives cantaloupe and mango their characteristic color.

2   cups chopped cantaloupe (about 1 small)
1½ cups chopped mango (about 2 medium)
1   tablespoon lemon juice
½   teaspoon almond extract
1   cup fat-free half-and-half
¼   cup cream of coconut
1   tablespoon plus 1 teaspoon flaked coconut, toasted

Place first 6 ingredients in a blender; process until smooth, stopping once to scrape down sides. Cover and chill 1 hour.
To serve, ladle 1 cup soup into individual bowls; sprinkle each with 1 teaspoon toasted coconut.
Yield: 4 servings (serving size: 1 cup).

Per Serving: Calories **143** Fat **4.2g** (sat **3.5g**) Protein **1.7g** Carbohydrate **25.3g** Fiber **2.3g**
Cholesterol **0mg** Iron **0.4mg** Sodium **53mg** Calcium **38mg**
Exchanges: 1½ Fruit, 1 Fat

Gazpacho

prep: 15 minutes   chill: 1 hour

Serve this refreshing chilled soup, loaded with good-for-you foods such as canned tomatoes and tomato juice, for a light summer supper. Tomato products contain the nutrient lycopene, which may help prevent certain types of cancer.

1   (14½-ounce) can diced tomatoes with garlic and onions, undrained and chilled
1   cup vegetable juice, chilled
¾   cup coarsely chopped seeded peeled cucumber (1 large)
½   cup chopped green bell pepper (1 small)
⅓   cup chopped green onions (about 2)
1   tablespoon red wine vinegar
1   teaspoon olive oil
1   garlic clove, minced
⅛   teaspoon hot sauce
¼   teaspoon salt
⅛   teaspoon freshly ground black pepper
12   fat-free herb-seasoned croutons

Combine first 11 ingredients in a large bowl. Cover and chill 1 hour.
To serve, ladle soup into individual serving bowls. Top each serving with 3 croutons.
Yield: 4 servings (serving size: 1 cup).

Per Serving: Calories 83 Fat **1.5g** (sat **0.2g**) Protein **2.6g** Carbohydrate **15.3g** Fiber **1.3g**
Cholesterol **0mg** Iron **1.3mg** Sodium **804mg** Calcium **33mg**
Exchanges: 3 Vegetable

Corn, Leek, and Potato Chowder

prep: 3 minutes   cook: 14 minutes

Add a romaine lettuce salad and whole wheat rolls, and you can put a complete meal on the table in a flash.

Cooking spray
1   cup sliced leek (about 2 small)
2   cups frozen hash brown potatoes with onions and peppers
        (such as Ore-Ida Potatoes O'Brien), thawed
1   (10-ounce) package frozen whole-kernel corn, thawed
½   teaspoon salt
¼   teaspoon freshly ground black pepper
2½ cups fat-free milk
1   cup (4 ounces) preshredded reduced-fat Cheddar cheese

Heat a large saucepan coated with cooking spray over medium-high heat. Add leek, and sauté 2 minutes. Add hash brown potatoes and next 3 ingredients; cook 3 minutes, stirring occasionally.

Add milk to potato mixture; bring to a boil. Reduce heat; simmer, uncovered, 8 minutes, stirring often.

To serve, ladle chowder into individual bowls; top evenly with cheese.

Yield: 4 servings (serving size: 1 cup).

Per Serving: Calories **250**   Fat **6.2g** (sat **3.4g**)   Protein **17.2g**   Carbohydrate **34.0g**   Fiber **3.3g**
Cholesterol **21mg**   Iron **1.2mg**   Sodium **603mg**   Calcium **431mg**
Exchanges: 1½ Starch, 1 Vegetable, 2 Lean Meat

Italian Bean Soup

prep: 10 minutes   cook: 18 minutes

Beans are a great source of cholesterol-lowering soluble fiber. Serve this heart-healthy soup with soft garlic breadsticks and a simple salad tossed with fat-free Italian dressing.

Cooking spray
1   cup chopped green bell pepper (about 1 large)
1   cup chopped onion (1 medium)
2   (16-ounce) cans navy beans, rinsed and drained
1   (14-ounce) can fat-free, less-sodium chicken broth
1   (14½-ounce) can diced Italian-style tomatoes, undrained
1   tablespoon commercial pesto

Heat a Dutch oven coated with cooking spray over medium-high heat. Add bell pepper and onion; cook 8 minutes or until onion is tender. **Add** beans and remaining 3 ingredients. Bring to a boil, reduce heat, and simmer, uncovered, 10 minutes.
Yield: 4 servings (serving size: 1½ cups).

Per Serving: Calories **228**   Fat **2.8g** (sat **0.5g**)   Protein **11.9g**   Carbohydrate **39.6g**   Fiber **7.2g**
Cholesterol **0mg**   Iron **4.7mg**   Sodium **1,223mg**   Calcium **162mg**
Exchanges: 2 Starch, 2 Vegetable, ½ Very Lean Meat

Minestrone

prep: 3 minutes   cook: 17 minutes

In Italian, minestrone *means "big soup." This hearty, "big soup" boasts the traditional pasta, beans, and vegetables.*

2   teaspoons olive oil
2   garlic cloves, minced
3   (14.5-ounce) cans fat-free, less-sodium chicken broth
        (such as Swanson's Natural Goodness)
1   (16-ounce) package frozen Italian-style vegetables
1   (16-ounce) can pinto beans, rinsed and drained
1   (14.5-ounce) can diced Italian-style tomatoes, undrained
3   ounces uncooked tubetti or other small tubular pasta (about
        ¾ cup)
1½ teaspoons dried Italian seasoning
3   tablespoons plus 1 teaspoon freshly grated Parmesan cheese

Heat oil in a large saucepan over medium heat. Add garlic, and cook
1 minute or until lightly browned. Stir in chicken broth and next
5 ingredients. Bring to a boil; reduce heat, and simmer, uncovered,
15 minutes or until pasta is tender.
To serve, ladle into individual bowls, and sprinkle each serving with
1 teaspoon Parmesan cheese.
Yield: 10 servings (serving size: 1 cup).

Per Serving: Calories **143**   Fat **1.9g** (sat **0.5g**)   Protein **6.2g**   Carbohydrate **23.9g**   Fiber **3.3g**
Cholesterol **1mg**   Iron **1.9mg**   Sodium **509mg**   Calcium **67mg**
Exchanges: 1 Starch, 2 Vegetable

Beefy Minestrone

prep: 2 minutes   cook: 15 minutes

Deli-sliced roast beef adds a unique twist to the traditional Italian minestrone.

2   (14¼-ounce) cans fat-free, no-salt-added beef broth (such as
      Health Valley)
1   (14.5-ounce) can no-salt-added stewed tomatoes, undrained
3   ounces uncooked ditalini pasta (about ⅔ cup)
1   large zucchini
1   (16-ounce) can cannellini beans or other white beans, rinsed
      and drained
2   teaspoons dried Italian seasoning
8   ounces thinly sliced rare deli roast beef, diced

Combine first 3 ingredients in a large saucepan; cover and bring to a boil over high heat.

While pasta mixture comes to a boil, cut zucchini in half lengthwise, and slice. Add zucchini, beans, and Italian seasoning to pasta; cover, reduce heat, and simmer 6 minutes. Add beef, and cook 4 minutes or until pasta is tender.

Yield: 6 servings (serving size: 1½ cups).

Per Serving: Calories **157**   Fat **1.8g** (sat **0.7g**)   Protein **13.5g**   Carbohydrate **20.7g**   Fiber **4.4g**   Cholesterol **20mg**   Iron **2.4mg**   Sodium **303mg**   Calcium **49mg**
Exchanges: 1 Starch, 1 Vegetable, 1 Very Lean Meat

Roasted Chicken Noodle Soup

prep: 3 minutes   cook: 15 minutes

For the chicken in this recipe, use leftover roasted chicken or pick up rotisserie chicken at your grocer's deli. Serve with carrot sticks and saltine crackers.

Cooking spray
2   cups frozen cubed hash brown potatoes
1½ cups frozen onion and pepper seasoning blend (such as
        McKenzie's)
2   (14-ounce) cans fat-free, less-sodium chicken broth
2   ounces uncooked wide egg noodles (about 1 cup)
½   teaspoon salt
⅛   teaspoon dried thyme
1   cup diced roasted chicken breast
1   cup evaporated fat-free milk

Heat a large saucepan coated with cooking spray over medium-high heat. Add hash brown potatoes and seasoning blend; sauté 3 minutes. Add broth and next 3 ingredients; bring to a boil. Reduce heat, and simmer, partially covered, 7 minutes. Add chicken and milk; cook 5 minutes or until noodles are tender.
Yield: 5 servings (serving size: 1 cup).

Per Serving: Calories **167**   Fat **1.9g** (sat **0.5g**)   Protein **14.8g**   Carbohydrate **21.1g**   Fiber **0.6g**
Cholesterol **35mg**   Iron **1.0mg**   Sodium **525mg**   Calcium **156mg**
Exchanges: 1½ Starch, 2 Very Lean Meat

Mexican Chicken Soup

prep: 8 minutes   cook: 9 minutes

Put some zip into your chicken soup with the tastes of Mexico.

5   cups fat-free, less-sodium chicken broth
1½   cups thick and chunky salsa
1   (9-ounce) package frozen diced cooked chicken breast, thawed
1   cup no-salt-added black beans, rinsed and drained
1   cup instant rice, uncooked
¼   cup chopped fresh cilantro
2   tablespoons fresh lime juice (about 2 limes)
¾   cup coarsely crushed baked tortilla chips

Bring broth and salsa to a boil in a large, heavy saucepan over high heat. Add chicken, beans, and rice; cover, reduce heat to low, and cook 4 minutes or until rice is tender. Remove from heat; stir in cilantro and lime juice.

To serve, ladle evenly into individual bowls. Sprinkle each serving with 2 tablespoons chips.

Yield: 6 servings.

Per Serving: Calories **245**   Fat **3.6g** (sat **0.9g**)   Protein **25.6g**   Carbohydrate **26.5g**   Fiber **2.5g**
Cholesterol **49mg**   Iron **2.4mg**   Sodium **816mg**   Calcium **33mg**
Exchanges: 1½ Starch, 3 Very Lean Meat

Chicken Gumbo *(photo, page 6)*

prep: 2 minutes   cook: 14 minutes

Ask five Cajuns which kind of meat makes the best gumbo, and you'll get five different answers. We think chicken is the perfect ingredient for this Louisiana favorite. Serve this quick gumbo over cooked instant rice.

1   teaspoon olive oil
1   (10-ounce) package frozen onion and pepper seasoning blend
      (such as McKenzie's)
2   tablespoons all-purpose flour
1   cup fat-free, less-sodium chicken broth
¼   teaspoon hot sauce
1   (14.5-ounce) can Cajun-style stewed tomatoes with pepper, garlic,
      and Cajun spices, undrained
1   (10-ounce) package frozen sliced okra
1½ cups frozen diced cooked chicken breast

Heat olive oil in a large nonstick skillet over medium-high heat; add seasoning blend, and sauté 3 minutes. Add flour, stirring well. Add chicken broth, hot sauce, and tomatoes; cook 3 minutes or until mixture is slightly thickened. Add okra and chicken; cover and cook 8 minutes or until okra is tender.

Yield: 5 servings (serving size: 1 cup).

Per Serving: Calories **164**   Fat **3.1g** (sat **0.6g**)   Protein **16.8g**   Carbohydrate **16.8g**   Fiber **2.0g**
Cholesterol **33mg**   Iron **1.1mg**   Sodium **462mg**   Calcium **67mg**
Exchanges: 3 Vegetable, 2 Very Lean Meat

Veggie Sandwiches with Beer-Cheese Sauce

prep: 5 minutes   cook: 8 minutes

Have plenty of napkins on hand when you serve these cheesy, juicy sandwiches; they're messy but worth it. Serve with fresh pineapple spears and strawberries.

4   (2-ounce) onion rolls
Cooking spray
1   (8-ounce) package presliced mushrooms
1½ cups sliced zucchini (about 1 medium)
3   ounces light processed cheese (such as Velveeta), cubed
3   tablespoons light beer
⅛   teaspoon ground red pepper

Preheat oven to 350°.
Wrap onion rolls in aluminum foil, and bake at 350° for 5 to 7 minutes or until warm.
While rolls bake, heat a large nonstick skillet coated with cooking spray over medium-high heat. Add mushrooms and zucchini, and cook 5 minutes or until vegetables are tender, stirring often.
Place cheese and beer in a small saucepan; cook over medium heat, stirring constantly, until cheese melts and mixture is smooth. Stir in pepper. Remove from heat.
Spoon one-fourth of vegetable mixture onto bottom half of each warm onion roll. Spoon about 2 tablespoons cheese sauce over vegetables; top with remaining roll half. Serve immediately.
Yield: 4 servings.

Per Serving: Calories **221**   Fat **5.2g** (sat **2.6g**)   Protein **12.3g**   Carbohydrate **31.6g**   Fiber **2.0g**
Cholesterol **8mg**   Iron **0.9mg**   Sodium **569mg**   Calcium **11mg**
Exchanges: 2 Starch, 1 Medium-Fat Meat

• vegetarian •

French Onion Sandwiches

prep: 3 minutes   cook: 10 minutes

*Shave thin slices from an onion with a very sharp chef's knife, or cut
the onion in half and push slowly through the slicing blade of a food
processor. These sandwiches are terrific with tomato soup.*

8   (1-ounce) slices French bread
Cooking spray
2   teaspoons reduced-calorie stick margarine
1   large onion, very thinly sliced
1½ tablespoons brown sugar
1   cup (4 ounces) shredded reduced-fat Swiss cheese

Preheat oven to 375°.
Arrange bread slices on a baking sheet. Bake at 375° for 8 minutes
or until lightly toasted. Remove from oven, and leave bread slices on
baking sheet.
While bread toasts, coat a large heavy saucepan with cooking spray;
add margarine, and place over high heat until margarine melts. Add
onion, and sauté 3 minutes or until onion is tender. Add brown sugar,
and cook 5 minutes or until onion is tender and browned, stirring often.
Preheat broiler.
Spoon onion mixture evenly on bread slices; top with cheese. Broil 2
minutes. Serve immediately.
Yield: 4 servings (serving size: 2 slices).

Per Serving: Calories **314**   Fat **8.3g** (sat **3.2g**)   Protein **16.0g**   Carbohydrate **43.4g**   Fiber **1.6g**
Cholesterol **20mg**   Iron **1.6mg**   Sodium **447mg**   Calcium **372mg**
Exchanges: 3 Starch, 1 High-Fat Meat

Sweet Pepper Sourdough Melts

prep: 5 minutes   cook: 9 minutes

Frozen vegetables are as nutritious as their fresh counterparts—just watch out for those with cheese and butter sauces.

1   (8-ounce) sourdough bread baguette
1   tablespoon plus 1 teaspoon commercial pesto
1   (16-ounce) package frozen pepper stir-fry (such as Birds Eye),
      thawed and drained
Olive oil-flavored cooking spray
2   garlic cloves, minced
¼   teaspoon salt
¼   teaspoon black pepper
1   cup (4 ounces) preshredded part-skim mozzarella cheese

Preheat broiler.
Cut bread in half lengthwise, then in half crosswise, forming 4 portions.
Place bread, cut side up, on an ungreased baking sheet; broil 3 minutes or until lightly toasted. Spread evenly with pesto; set aside.
Heat a large nonstick skillet over medium-high heat. Coat peppers with cooking spray. Add pepper stir-fry, garlic, salt, and pepper; sauté 3 minutes. Spoon about ½ cup pepper mixture over each toasted bread portion; top each with ¼ cup cheese. Broil 3 minutes or until cheese melts. Serve immediately.
Yield: 4 servings.

Per Serving: Calories **305**   Fat **9.2g** (sat **3.8g**)   Protein **14.4g**   Carbohydrate **40.6g**   Fiber **4.7g**
Cholesterol **17mg**   Iron **2.3mg**   Sodium **730mg**   Calcium **271mg**
Exchanges: 2 Starch, 2 Vegetable, ½ Medium-Fat Meat, 1 Fat

Roast Beef-Feta
Pita Pockets

prep: 12 minutes

For a lower-sodium sandwich use leftover cooked roast beef instead of sliced deli meat. Serve with fresh pear wedges.

½   cup plus 2 tablespoons chopped seeded cucumber
⅓   cup fat-free ranch dressing
¼   cup (1 ounce) crumbled feta cheese
4   green leaf lettuce leaves
2   (6-inch) pitas, cut in half
6   ounces very thinly sliced deli roast beef

Combine cucumber, dressing, and cheese in a small bowl, stirring well. **Place** 1 lettuce leaf into each pita half; add 1½ ounces roast beef to each pita pocket. Spoon cucumber mixture evenly into each pocket. Serve immediately.

Yield: 4 servings (serving size: 1 filled pita half).

Per Serving: Calories **187**   Fat **4.3g** (sat **3.3g**)   Protein **13.2g**   Carbohydrate **21.6g**   Fiber **2.6g**
Cholesterol **31mg**   Iron **1.0mg**   Sodium **821mg**   Calcium **97mg**
Exchanges: 1 Starch, 1 Vegetable, 1 Medium-Fat Meat

Slim Sloppy Joes *(photo, page 9)*

prep: 3 minutes   cook: 15 minutes

Eat like a kid again! These sloppy joes are sure to make you reminisce about your childhood. Best part, however, is that this comforting classic is a lot healthier than what mom used to serve.

1   pound ground round
1   cup chopped onion (about 1 medium)
¼   cup ketchup
2   tablespoons unprocessed oat bran
1   tablespoon low-sodium Worcestershire sauce
1   tablespoon prepared mustard
1   tablespoon lemon juice
1   (8-ounce) can no-salt-added tomato sauce
6   (1½-ounce) reduced-calorie hamburger buns, split and toasted

Heat a large nonstick skillet over medium-high heat. Add ground round and onion; cook until meat is browned, stirring until meat crumbles. Drain and return to pan.

Stir ketchup and next 5 ingredients into meat mixture; bring to a boil. Cover, reduce heat, and simmer 10 minutes, stirring often. Spoon mixture evenly over bottom halves of buns; cover with bun tops. Serve immediately.

Yield: 6 servings.

Per Serving: Calories **250**   Fat **5.9g** (sat **1.9g**)   Protein **22.0g**   Carbohydrate **29.6g**   Fiber **4.4g**
Cholesterol **43mg**   Iron **3.4mg**   Sodium **391mg**   Calcium **44mg**
Exchanges: 2 Starch, 2 Lean Meat

Mexico Joes

prep: 5 minutes   cook: 8 minutes

Mix the leftover taco seasoning with fat-free sour cream to serve with fajitas, or stir the seasoning into coarsely crushed cornflakes to use as a coating for oven-fried chicken. Serve with baked tortilla chips and carrot sticks.

Cooking spray
1   pound ground round
½   cup frozen chopped onion
1   (4.5-ounce) can chopped green chiles, undrained
2   tablespoons 40%-less-sodium taco seasoning
1   (8-ounce) can no-salt-added tomato sauce
6   (1½-ounce) hamburger buns, warmed

Heat a large nonstick skillet coated with cooking spray over medium-high heat. Add ground round and onion; cook 5 minutes until meat is browned and onion is tender, stirring to crumble meat. Add chiles, taco seasoning, and tomato sauce, stirring well. Cook over medium heat 3 to 4 minutes or until thoroughly heated, stirring often.

Spoon meat mixture evenly over bottom halves of buns; top with remaining bun halves. Serve immediately.

Yield: 6 servings.

Per Serving: Calories **284**   Fat **7.5g** (sat **1.9g**)   Protein **20.8g**   Carbohydrate **31.4g**   Fiber **1.2g**
Cholesterol **58mg**   Iron **2.6mg**   Sodium **357mg**   Calcium **27mg**
Exchanges: 2½ Starch, 2 Lean Meat

Italian Grilled Panini

prep: 5 minutes cook: 10 minutes

Panini *(or small bread in Italian) generally refers to a pressed sand-wich. This recipe is reminiscent of the American grilled cheese.*

8   (1-ounce) slices Vienna bread
6   ounces sliced reduced-sodium deli smoked ham
4   (¾-ounce) slices reduced-fat provolone cheese or part-skim
      mozzarella cheese
1   (7-ounce) bottle roasted red bell pepper, drained and cut into strips
Garlic-flavored cooking spray

Preheat oven to 450°.

Top 4 bread slices with ham, cheese, and pepper strips; top with remaining bread slices.

Coat both sides of sandwiches with cooking spray. Place sandwiches on an ungreased baking sheet. Bake at 450° for 5 minutes on each side or until bread is golden and cheese is melted. Serve immediately.

Yield: 4 servings.

Per Serving: Calories **272**   Fat **6.2g** (sat **2.3g**)   Protein **19.6g**   Carbohydrate **36.7g**   Fiber **2.0g**
Cholesterol **30mg**   Iron **2.1mg**   Sodium **846mg**   Calcium **295mg**
Exchanges: 2 Starch, 1 Vegetable, 2 Lean Meat

Shrimp Rémoulade Rolls

prep: 10 minutes   cook: 5 minutes

You can save some cooking time by having the shrimp steamed at the grocery store. Serve with coleslaw.

3   cups water
40   medium shrimp, peeled and deveined (about 1 pound)
¼   cup Creole mustard
3   tablespoons light mayonnaise
3   tablespoons dill pickle relish
¼   teaspoon freshly ground black pepper
½   (16-ounce) package twin French bread loaves
6   green leaf lettuce leaves

Preheat oven to 425°.

Bring water to a boil in a medium saucepan; add shrimp, and cook 3 to 5 minutes or until shrimp are done.

While shrimp cooks, combine mustard and next 3 ingredients, and set aside. Split bread loaf in half horizontally; place halves back together, and wrap loaf in aluminum foil. Bake at 425° for 5 minutes or until heated.

Drain shrimp well; rinse with cold water. Coarsely chop shrimp; add to mustard mixture, stirring well.

Line each cut half of bread loaf with 3 lettuce leaves. Spoon shrimp mixture evenly over lettuce. Cut each half diagonally into 3 slices. Serve immediately.

Yield: 6 servings (serving size: 1 slice).

Per Serving: Calories **202**   Fat **4.2g** (sat **0.4g**)   Protein **16.8g**   Carbohydrate **22.6g**   Fiber **1.1g**
Cholesterol **120mg**   Iron **2.8mg**   Sodium **610mg**   Calcium **44mg**
Exchanges: 1½ Starch, 2 Lean Meat

Fruited Chicken Salad Pitas

prep: 15 minutes

These pitas are great for lunch or for a light dinner. Add fat-free pretzels to round out the meal.

⅓   cup fat-free mayonnaise
¼   teaspoon salt
2½ cups chopped cooked chicken breast (about 1 pound)
1   cup halved seedless red grapes
1½ tablespoons chopped pecans, toasted
1   (11-ounce) can mandarin oranges in light syrup, drained
6   small green leaf lettuce leaves
3   (6-inch) whole wheat pitas, cut in half

Combine first 5 ingredients in a medium bowl, stirring well. Gently stir in oranges.
Place 1 lettuce leaf in each pita pocket half. Spoon ¾ cup chicken salad into each pita half. Serve immediately.
Yield: 6 servings (serving size: 1 filled pita half).

Per Serving: Calories **208**   Fat **3.8g** (sat **0.7g**)   Protein **18.5g**   Carbohydrate **23.0g**   Fiber **2.7g**
Cholesterol **46mg**   Iron **1.5mg**   Sodium **448mg**   Calcium **34mg**
Exchanges: 1 Starch, ½ Fruit, 2 Very Lean Meat

Smoked Turkey and Avocado Bagels

prep: 15 minutes

Bagels are a healthy alternative to some high-fat breads, but make sure you watch portion sizes. Look for bagels that are about the size of the palm of your hand. Some bakery bagels can add up to four bread servings.

½   pound smoked turkey breast, finely chopped
⅓   cup chopped avocado (about ½)
½   teaspoon lemon juice
⅓   cup finely shredded carrot
2   tablespoons creamy mustard blend (such as Dijonnaise)
⅛   teaspoon freshly ground black pepper
2   fresh poppy seed bagels, halved and toasted
½   red onion, sliced and separated into rings
¼   cup alfalfa sprouts (about ½ pint)

Combine first 6 ingredients in a large bowl. Spread ½ cup turkey mixture on top of each bagel half. Top bagels evenly with onion rings and alfalfa sprouts. Serve immediately.

Yield: 4 servings (serving size: 1 topped bagel half).

Per Serving: Calories **312**   Fat **4.1g** (sat **0.8g**)   Protein **16.8g**   Carbohydrate **37.5g**   Fiber **3.0g**
Cholesterol **24mg**   Iron **2.7mg**   Sodium **925mg**   Calcium **60mg**
Exchanges: 2 Starch, 1 Vegetable, 1 Lean Meat

Garden Vegetable Wraps

prep: 8 minutes   cook: 2 minutes

You can substitute one 7-ounce bottle of roasted red bell peppers for ¾ cup red bell pepper. Just remember that the sodium will be higher.

2   slices turkey bacon
4   (10-inch) flour tortillas
¼   cup light cream cheese
20   fresh basil or spinach leaves, cut into thin strips
2½   cups coarsely chopped tomato (about 2 large)
¾   cup chopped red bell pepper (about 1 small)
¼   teaspoon freshly ground black pepper

Place bacon slices in microwave; cook at HIGH 2 minutes or until crisp. Crumble and set aside.

Spread 1 side of each tortilla with 1 tablespoon cream cheese. Layer bacon, basil, tomato, and red pepper evenly over cream cheese; sprinkle each with black pepper.

Roll up tortillas, jelly roll fashion; wrap bottom halves of sandwiches with parchment paper or aluminum foil. Serve immediately.

Yield: 4 servings.

Per Serving: Calories **194** Fat **6.1g** (sat **2.1g**) Protein **6.0g** Carbohydrate **24.2g** Fiber **2.9g**
Cholesterol **13mg** Iron **0.9mg** Sodium **461mg** Calcium **27mg**
Exchanges: 1½ Starch, 1 Fat

index

metric equivalents

The information in the following charts is provided to help cooks outside the United States successfully use the recipes in this book. All equivalents are approximate.

Equivalents for Different Types of Ingredients

Standard Cup	Fine Powder (ex. flour)	Grain (ex. rice)	Granular (ex. sugar)	Liquid Solids (ex. butter)	Liquid (ex. milk)
1	140 g	150 g	190 g	200 g	240 ml
¾	105 g	113 g	143 g	150 g	180 ml
⅔	93 g	100 g	125 g	133 g	160 ml
½	70 g	75 g	95 g	100 g	120 ml
⅓	47 g	50 g	63 g	67 g	80 ml
¼	35 g	38 g	48 g	50 g	60 ml
⅛	18 g	19 g	24 g	25 g	30 ml

Liquid Ingredients by Volume

¼ tsp			1 ml
½ tsp			2 ml
1 tsp			5 ml
3 tsp = 1 tbls	= ½ fl oz	=	15 ml
2 tbls = ⅛ cup	= 1 fl oz	=	30 ml
4 tbls = ¼ cup	= 2 fl oz	=	60 ml
5⅓ tbls = ⅓ cup	= 3 fl oz	=	80 ml
8 tbls = ½ cup	= 4 fl oz	=	120 ml
10⅔ tbls = ⅔ cup	= 5 fl oz	=	160 ml
12 tbls = ¾ cup	= 6 fl oz	=	180 ml
16 tbls = 1 cup	= 8 fl oz	=	240 ml
1 pt = 2 cups	= 16 fl oz	=	480 ml
1 qt = 4 cups	= 32 fl oz	=	960 ml
	33 fl oz	= 1000 ml	= 1 liter

Dry Ingredients by Weight
(To convert ounces to grams, multiply the number of ounces by 30.)

1 oz	=	¹⁄₁₆ lb	=	30 g
4 oz	=	¼ lb	=	120 g
8 oz	=	½ lb	=	240 g
12 oz	=	¾ lb	=	360 g
16 oz	=	1 lb	=	480 g

Length
(To convert inches to centimeters, multiply the number of inches by 2.5.)

1 in =	2.5 cm
6 in = ½ ft	= 15 cm
12 in = 1 ft	= 30 cm
36 in = 3 ft = 1 yd	= 90 cm
40 in =	100 cm = 1 m

Cooking/Oven Temperatures

	Fahrenheit	Celsius	Gas Mark
Freeze Water	32° F	0° C	
Room Temperature	68° F	20° C	
Boil Water	212° F	100° C	
Bake	325° F	160° C	3
	350° F	180° C	4
	375° F	190° C	5
	400° F	200° C	6
	425° F	220° C	7
	450° F	230° C	8
Broil	Broil	Broil	Grill